ROUGH AND SMOOTH
COLLIES

STELLA CLARK

RINGPRESS

RINGPRESS

Published by Ringpress Books Ltd,
Spirella House, Bridge Road,
Letchworth, Herts, SG6 4ET

Discounts available for bulk orders
Contact the Special Sales Manager at
the above address. Telephone (0462) 674177

Distributed to the Book Trade in the United Kingdom by
Bookpoint Ltd.
39 Milton Park, Abingdon, Oxon OX14 4TD
Telephone 0235 835001

Distributed in the United States Of America and Canada by
Seven Hills Book Distributors
49 Central Avenue, Cincinnati, Ohio 45202.

First Published 1993
© 1993 STELLA CLARK

ISBN 0 948955 82 1

Printed and bound in Singapore
by Kyodo Printing Co

CONTENTS

This book is dedicated to my husband, Leslie.

ACKNOWLEDGEMENTS

I would like to thank the following people for all the help given to me while writing this book – delving into past records for old snips of history, or for photographs of the Rough and Smooth Collie.

To Judith White, who introduced me into the world of Smooth Collies; if I had not seen her trio of sable and white Smooths all those years ago, this book might not have been written – well, at least, not by me! To Mrs Floss Chapman for allowing me to have the beautiful Rough Collie, Emma, the foundation bitch of my kennel, from whom all my Collies – Rough and Smooth – are descended.

To Mrs Ada Bishop for all her kind interest in this book, and for supplying me with some fascinating photographs. To Mr Roy Baker for allowing me to pick his brains and reprint some of his written work on the Smooth Collie. To Lyn Westby for burning the midnight oil to sort through mountains of old and interesting articles. To Mr Lyn Howells for his magnificent photographs of today's top winning Smooth Collies – such a dedicated Smooth fancier and an expert photographer. To Mia Ejerstad, of the famous Steadlyn Collies, for her truly outstanding drawings that have never been seen in Britain before. I am indebted to Mia and Bernardo for all their help, and also some magnificent photographs of their dogs.

A special thanks to my boss, Mr David Flatt DVM (Toronto) MRCVS, for his help in reviewing the health and general care section, and to his assistant, Didier Poot, BVSc. MRCVS (Pretoria), for his help on OCD; I am grateful to him for putting up with my endless questions.

Last, but not at all least, to my family who have hardly seen me over the last year – and a very special thank-you to my husband Leslie for the endless cups of coffee!

INTRODUCTION

When I was a child, we had an odd assortment of dogs in our family, and my father showed a few Pekes, with some success. One of my favourite dogs was an old-fashioned Bull Terrier called 'Patch' – he was white all over, with just one black patch. What a character this dog was – we used to dress him up, put him in a pram and park him at the bottom of our road, where he sat for hours! Towards the end of the war, we took in a dog that we found wandering, following a bombing raid in London. He was a beautiful red colour, and we found out much later that he was a Collie-Chow cross. He looked very Collie-like, but had a short, dense, red coat, and he had a black tongue. We did not know his real name, so we called him 'Roxy' after a cinema that had been bombed, near our home. At first, he would eat nothing. We put it down to the fact he was missing his owners, so we tried all sorts of food, but all to no avail. One day, we had some pasta and tomatoes for supper; he went round and round in a big circle, barking and asking for some of the food – we found out later that his past owners were Italians! He was a super companion to us children, following us to school, and even waiting outside until we came out, to follow us home again. My father was an avid snooker player, and Roxy was the only dog I knew who was allowed in the snooker hall. When my father was late home for his Sunday lunch, my Mother used to send Roxy to fetch him home.

I left home in 1950 to start a career in the hairdressing trade, and I did not have any dogs of my own at the time. However, my landlady bred Yorkshire Terriers, and I had as many as twenty in my room on some occasions. I enjoyed the company of Miss Noakes, and I learnt a lot about dogs from her. I married my husband, Leslie, in 1956, and at that time I had my own hairdressing salon in London, and so I was unable to keep dogs for a while. Then, in 1967, I fell in love with the most beautiful Rough Collie I had ever seen. He was a very large dog – at least twenty-six inches at the shoulder – but what a magnificent sight he was! His coat was the colour of burnished copper, and he had a full white collar and mane, almost down to his toes. He took my breath away, and I decided that I had to have him. His name was Deloraine Dinner Jacket, bred by Mrs Floss Chapman, and at that time he was owned by Mrs Anne Parlour of the Corena prefix. He was sired by Mrs F. Jeffreys' Clanayre Coral Diver and was out of Deloraine Corena Christaly. He had all the well-known names in his pedigree – Jefsfire, Danvis, Ladypark – and the beautiful Ch. Starlet of Glenmist. However, fate played a cruel part, and this dog proved to be sterile. I did not show him, but he lived a full and happy life till he died of a stroke at the age of ten years. 'Manzie', as he was known, was my introduction to the wonderful world of the Rough Collie.

As I was impressed with the Rough Collies bred by Mrs Chapman, I went to her to buy a Rough Collie to show. I saw the lovely bitch, Deloraine Dilemma, at one of the London Collie shows in

1969, and I asked if I could buy her. After a wait that seemed endless, Mrs Chapman telephoned to say I could pick her up, and every dog, Rough or Smooth, that has come out of my kennel is related to this bitch. She was mainly Ladypark-bred, with Pattingham lines. So the seed was sown; I was hooked, and I still am, to this day, madly in love with this beautiful breed. I mated Deloraine Dilemma to the 'man of the day', Ch. Ramsey of Rokeby, and among the resulting litter was Astrellita Alona. When Alona was mated to Ch. Beaublade Barrister, she produced my best Collie of all time – the uncrowned Astrellita Able Seaman. What a dog he was! A real gentleman, and so handsome and proud. He sired some lovely progeny including the Smooth

Manzie: my first Rough Collie.

Champions Ch. Astrellita Pot Black and Ch. Astrellita Midnight Dynamo. In fact, Dynamo went out to Australia to take his title there, and he produced some outstanding stock for Mr and Mrs Watson.

When Able Seaman died of old age at nearly fourteen years old, he left a big, gaping hole that has never been filled. Perhaps, one day, another 'Barney' will come along to take his place. However, from that time onwards I decided to concentrate on Smooth Collies, and I have got more involved with them as the years have gone by. Some very nice Roughs have left Astrellita to win well for their new owners. They include the beautiful blue, Astrellita Amaranthine (two CCs, four RCCs), Astrellita Amy (one CC), and Astrellita Apple Blossom and Astrellita Cherry Blossom, both Reserve CC winners. It is a few years since I have shown a Rough Collie, but I have not forsaken them, as I have judged the breed in many countries, such as Finland, Sweden, Austria, Hungary, Italy, Switzerland and Luxemburg, and I am sure I shall return to the Rough ring with a new Rough Collie at some later stage.

I first made up my mind to have a Smooth Collie after seeing Judith White show her three beautiful, sable and white Smooth Collies at a Collie club show, where I was exhibiting my Rough Collies. I found these three Smooths of such outstanding beauty that I could not take my eyes from them. They were the three famous sisters Ch. Dancerwood Freelance, Dancerwood Dellaware and Dancerwood Slightly Saucy. I tried to buy the sable bitch Dellaware, who, in my opinion, carried the best head I have ever seen in a Rough or a Smooth Collie. However, I was unsuccessful, and my search for a Smooth Collie of this quality continued for some time, but I could not find one to match 'Della'. Four years later, I was approached by Mrs White who asked if I was still interested in having Della – and I needed no second asking! From that day Della was the light of my life. She lived as a house dog, and I found her the most enchanting companion – I never tired of looking at her beautiful head and her outstanding soft, gentle eyes, and she was to have a tremendous influence on my breeding programme

My great breakthrough in breeding Smooth Collies came in 1976 when I received a telephone

*Astrellita Able
Seaman, pictured
at thirteen years of
age.*

Jean Kenny.

call from a Mrs Brenda Trundley, who ran the Treewood kennels of Smooth Collies. She told me that she had a litter of Smooth Collie puppies that needed rearing, as the owner – Mrs Judith White – had been involved in a car accident and had been taken to hospital. I swiftly made arrangements to collect the litter. And that fateful day changed my life, for that litter included the famous sisters – my own Ch. Dancerwood Bewitched of Astrellita, and Ch. Dancerwood Crown Jewel, bought by Mr Roy Baker – and the dog that was to prove an outstanding sire in Sweden, Dancerwood Court Jester. All three were tricolours, and they were to have a great influence on the breed. They are behind many of today's top winning smooth Collies in Britain and overseas.

I mated Della to her nephew, Dancerwood Court Jester, before he went to Sweden. In the resulting litter she produced the tricolour Ch. Astrellita The Gunslinger of Newarp, bought by Mrs Pat Lister, who campaigned him to his title and to win the CC at Crufts. 'Cody', as he was known, sired Pat's Ch. Newarp Silver Moonlight. When Moonlight was mated to Ch. Sylbeq Draught Guinness at Foxearth, the result was the record winning bitch Ch. Newarp Silver Moonbeam. This combination mating worked so well that Della was mated to Jester again, and this time she produced a very pretty sable bitch, Astrellita Love Affair. She was bought by Trevor and Brigit Harward, and later produced the well-known, handsome, sable dog, Ch. Foxearth Goldfever and his tricolour brother, Champion Foxearth Fenix. Goldfever went on to sire so many outstanding winners, including the breed's most prolific sire (since Black Hawk of Kasan – the American Smooth Collie), Ch. Sylbeq Draught Guinness Foxearth. This truly outstanding dog was bred by Roy Baker and his partner Mike Vincent.

*Ch. Dancerwood
Bewitched of
Astrellita:
winner of ten CCs.*

Just before leaving for Sweden, Jester mated one of my Rough Collie bitches, Silveretta of Astrellita. She was the most outstanding blue, and from that mating came Ch. Astrellita The Silversmith, who, after a successful show career – including Best of Breed at Crufts in 1983 – was voted Top Smooth Collie of the Year in 1988, at the age of almost eleven years. He was a grand dog, with a wonderful, gentle nature. He had fan mail from all over the world, with Smooth Collie lovers writing to ask for photographs of him. It was a very sad day when he died, but I have many happy memories, and I can see his likeness in his grandchildren, now in the ring. 'Smithy' sired Ch. Foxearth the Blacksmith and Ch. Foxearth the Tinsmith. Jester was full brother to my own Ch. Dancerwood Bewitched of Astrellita, who won ten CCs, including Best of Breed at Crufts in 1979. I remember her winning Best in Show at the London Collie Championship Show when over four hundred entries were on show. 'Mandy', as she was known, also takes her place on the roll of honour as the dam of that illustrious blue bitch, Ch. Astrellita Blue Movie of Glenmist, winner of thirty CCs. She was sold as a puppy of eight weeks to Frank and Lillian Mitchell of the Glenmist Collies, and not only did she do them well in the ring, she also won the award of Top Smooth Collie Bitch two years running, and won the Top Brood Bitch as well. Her offspring included: Ch. Glenmist Rough Diamond, Ch. Glenmist Blue Lodestone, Ch. Glenmist Blue Diamond, and Ch. Glenmist Movie Maestro.

Chapter One

ORIGINS OF THE ROUGH AND SMOOTH COLLIE

The early origins of the Rough and Smooth Collie are somewhat obscure, and no real proof of their exact origins can be found. Shepherd dogs have been around for centuries, and the name 'shepherd dog' covered dogs of many shapes and sizes. As long as there have been flocks of sheep and herds of cattle, there has been the shepherd-type dog. It has been said that when the Romans invaded Britain they brought sheep and cattle to feed their armies, and they also brought dogs with them in order to guard the livestock. When attempting to search for the specific origins of the Collie breed, even the name 'Collie' does not help us much, as it has been spelt in many ways over the years. In early books on 'shepherd' breeds, the word 'Coll' or 'Colley' was used to describe black dogs, dating from Anglo-Saxon times. The word 'Col' meant black, and the dogs were called after the black-faced sheep that were common at this time.

Despite the lack of detailed evidence, there is no doubt that the Collie is descended from these early shepherd-type dogs. Perhaps we should look to the North of England, where a dog was needed to assist in all weathers, working high in the hills. These dogs were smaller than today's Collies; they were more of the Border Collie type, having a broader head and shorter muzzle, with a more pronounced stop. These sheepdogs were intelligent, and the shepherds found them easy to train as they were biddable and eager to please. Records show that originally, the Smooth Collie was the result of mating the old black and white Collie with the Greyhound, and I am sure this must be true, as even today, we often see the odd Smooth Collie turn up with some of the hound-like traits, such as a tucked-up body, an over-long head and receding skull, and sometimes Smooths have very hound-like ears. The Smooth Collie is also much faster than the Rough. These Smooth Collies were more commonly found in the North of England in the early days; they were regarded more as working dogs, and always took second place to the more glamorous heavy-coated Rough Collie in the show ring. But up in the hills, shepherds needed dogs with smooth racey lines to climb the hills in bad weather, and they found the Smooth Collie more suitable for this work. Alas, throughout history, the Smooth Collies has always been regarded as the poor relation. That is, until now, when the Smooth Collie can hold its own in any competition, anywhere in the world, and it sometimes out-classes the Rough Collie by winning Best in Show at Collie Club shows.

In the early 1800s the breeding of Rough Collies was encouraged, and many changes took place which resulted in the Collie as we know it today. In the early days large sums of money changed hands – comparatively far more than current prices paid for puppies. Many top breeders sent stock to Collie fanciers in America, who were prepared to pay astronomical prices for the dogs they wanted. So the breed really took off, and from its humble, working origins, the beautiful Rough

The Smooth Collie by Norah Drummond. One of a series of six cards published by Raphael Tuck and Co., titled 'Scotch Collies'. English Kennel Club.

Old Cockie (1868) the first sable Rough Collie to take the show scene by storm, and Ch. Charlemagne (1879).

Collie was now in demand to grace the homes of grand families – and it was all set to take the dog show scene by storm. The first dog show was held in Newcastle in 1859; this show was for Setters and Pointers only. The City of Birmingham was the venue for the next show, held in the same year, but this was also confined to Sporting dogs. In 1860 the first classes for sheepdogs were held, and this classification included any dog that worked sheep. It was not until 1870 that separate classes were organised for Short-tailed Sheepdogs, and Rough and Short-coated Sheepdogs. Included in these classes were smooth-coated Shetland Sheepdogs, which were listed until they were written out of the Standard in 1914. There were very few early records, and even when the Kennel Club was formed in 1873, it was not compulsory to register dogs. The records that do exist show that Sheepdogs were a popular breed, and all shows put on classes with great success. Collies were still being shown in mixed classes along with all other Sheepdogs, and it was not

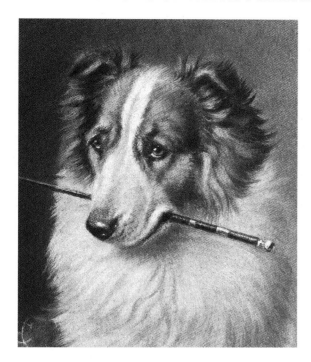

*Oscar: one of Queen
Victoria's Collies.*

until 1895 that the breed was designated as Collies Rough, and Collies Smooth, as it still is today. The distinct difference between the Rough and Smooth Collie can be seen in a print of the Collie show, held at the Royal Aquarium in 1885, featuring Mr W. Arkwright's famous Ch. Blue Ruin. In 1870, a show was held at the Crystal Palace in London, with scheduled classes for Sheepdogs Rough, and Sheepdogs Smooth – making a division between the two types of coat for the first time. At this show, the prize for best Smooth Collie was withheld due to lack of merit. The first Smooth Collie to win consistently in the show ring was a bitch called Fan, a blue, bred by Mr Mapplebeck. If Challenge Certificates had been on offer, Fan would certainly have been the very first Smooth Collie Champion. In fact, the first Smooth Champion was the tricolour dog, Ch. Guelt, born in 1873, sired by Captain out of a bitch named Nora. He was bred by a Mr Craig, but he was owned by Mr W. W. Thompson, who also owned Ch. Yarrow. Until 1871, all Collies – Rough and Smooth – were black and white, black and tan, or tricolour, until along came the Rough Collie, Old Cockie. Old Cockie created a sensation at the time, as he was the most magnificent sable colour, and he was responsible for changing the whole Collie scene. From then on, any colour sable – from red to mahogany – was all the rage, and was much sought after by Collie exhibitors. On a visit to Balmoral, Queen Victoria was most impressed when she saw Rough Collies working on her estates there. She brought several to her kennels, making the Rough Collie even more popular, and from a humble background the Rough Collie became a dog to covet. In 1873 the great Trefoil was born. He was a tricolour, with a wealth of coat, bred by Mr S. E. Shirley, one of the Kennel Club's founder members. Trefoil sired the great Ch. Charlemagne, and every winning Collie can trace its ancestry back to these dogs. Until 1890, the top winning Smooth Collies were black and tan, or black and white, or tricolour – although a lemon and white was shown with some success. The sable and white Smooth never became popular like the sable

Roughs, and even today, for some unknown reason, it is very difficult to make up a Smooth sable Champion. However, there were some well-known sables around in the early 1900s, such as Ch. Scorton Ladylove and the lovely Ch. Ellwyn Biddy. The colour 'black and tan' is never seen on Collies, Rough or Smooth, any more, but on occasions it can still be seen in the Shetland Sheepdog.

The Rough Collie became a separate breed in 1895; before this time they were regarded as Sheepdogs of either coat. In 1880 the Kennel Club devised a form of Breed Standard for the Collies, and this was revised in 1895 when the breed was called 'Rough, and Smooth coated Collies'. The Standard for both Collies was the same, with the exception of coat, and this Standard stood for many years. In my opinion, some of the finest Smooth Collies ever bred were from Rough/Smooth matings, and I see no reason why the English Kennel Club has decided to ban the mating of Rough and Smooth Collies on a breed that has such a small gene pool. This is a measure that is scheduled to take place in 1993, and there are many breeders who fear that this may have adverse effects on the Smooth Collie. This would be a tragedy when, at long last, the Smooth Collie is winning the recognition it so richly deserves in the show ring. When I came into the Smooth Collie breed in 1975, you could count on one hand the number of Smooth Collies entered at a show, and now the entries are over the one-hundred mark at the major shows.

Chapter Two

ROUGH COLLIE HISTORY

In the late 1880s some beautiful Rough Collies were exhibited. Ch. Christopher was sold to Mr Tom Stretch for £60, and was then resold for a staggering £1,000 to Mr Mitchell Harrison of Philadelphia – probably because his sire was the well-known Ch. Metchley Wonder. Before leaving Britain Ch. Christopher sired many well-known winners including Edgbaston Marvel, who, in turn, sired Ch. Southport Perfection and Ch. Southport Pilot. Tom Stretch, owner of the Ormskirk prefix, followed this deal up in 1894 by selling Ch. Ormskirk Emerald, bred by Mr W. P. Barnes, to Mr Megson for the total sum of £1,300 (this price also included the dog Edgbaston Marvel) – an amazing sum of money for the time. Tom was best known for his Rough Collies, with many of his dogs gracing the ring in Britain and America, but he also bred the Smooth Collie, Ch. Ormskirk Venice, who gained his title in 1906.

The Parbold kennels belonged to Mr Ainscough, who bred many Champions. His first Rough Collie to be made up was Ch. Parbold Rover, whose name was changed by his new owner, Mr Chance, and who was later exhibited as Ch. Great Alne Douglas. Ch. Balgreggie Hope, born in 1896, was the sire of Parbold Pinafore and grandsire of Ch. Parbold Piccolo. Piccolo proved to be an outstanding sire and his Champion offspring included Ch. Anfield Model, Ch. Parbold Purity and Ch. Ormskirk Olympian. Piccolo was exported to America, for an undisclosed sum, but in 1904 he went missing, and sadly he was never found – a great loss to the breed.

There were many famous Rough Collie breeders of this era, and there was an abundance of good stock in the ring such as Ch. Seedley Sapphire, Ch. Eden Extra and Ch. Eden Elegance. However, no history of the breed can be written without mentioning Mr R. Tait, Mr R. Lord – the proud owner of the Seedley prefix (many of his dogs crossing the Atlantic to the USA) – and Mr W. Stanfield, owner of the world famous Laund prefix. The foundation of any kennel lies in the bitches and the ability to produce sound stock, and Mr Stansfield obviously had this in mind when he acquired the bitch Pure Gem in 1908, as she was to be the foundation bitch of the Laund dynasty. She was sired by Seedley Squire out of Lady Temple. The first Laund Champion was born on March 22nd 1912. His name was Ch. Laund Limit, sired by Ch. Parbold Picador out of Laund Lily. I have seen photographs of this dog, and, in my opinion, he was a beautiful specimen of the breed. The Laund kennels were well-known before the outbreak of the First World War, and then went on to even greater success in the post-war period. In 1924 the kennel took four CCs at the Birmingham National Show: the Rough Collie winners were Int. Ch. Laund Lukeo and Laund Lucia, and the Smooth Collie winners were Ch. Fellman and Laund Latha. By 1948 Mr Stansfield had bred a total of fifty-nine Champions, with many of his dogs being exported to America to improve bloodlines and to form the foundation of new kennels.

*Ch. Metchley
Wonder, born in
1886.
He was the sire of
Ch. Christopher
who was sold to the
USA for £1,000.*

*Ch. Balgreggie
Hope, born in 1896,
sire of many
Champions.*

The 1914-18 war put a stop to the world of dogs as a whole, as food shortages were so bad that the Kennel Club placed a ban on all dog breeding by refusing to register puppies born after September 27th 1917. Dogs could only be bred under special licence, and this ban was not lifted until January 1919. Two dogs were born prior to the ban, and they were Champion Laund Logic and Champion Laund Legislator. After the war, a new era of breeders and exhibitors emerged, and the early 1920s saw the start of the Backwoods, Ashteads, Alphingtons, and the world famous Beulahs, Ladyparks, and the Westcarrs. Miss Clare Malony bred some of the finest blue merles in the history of the Collie – the colour of these Collies was sheer perfection. One of the best blue merles around at this time was the superb Ch. Westcarrs Blue Minoru, sired by the tricolour dog, Rifflesee Royalist.

Miss Phyllis M. Grey of the famous Ladypark Collies purchased her first brood bitch in 1922 from Fred Robson of the Eden prefix. Miss Grey bred her Collies for the sheer pleasure they gave her, and it was not until much later that she started to exhibit them. She purchased a bitch from Mrs Nadine George, who was a daughter of Ch. Beulahs Golden Futureson. This bitch, Beulahs

Tom Stretch, owner of the famous Ormskirk prefix, pictured in 1928.

Sheils Beulah's Golden Viceroy.

Golden Flora, was in due course mated to Mr Robson's Eden Examiner, and from this litter came the world-famous Ch. Lochinvar of Ladypark. This Collie went on to win Best of Breed at Crufts in 1951; he was also Best of Breed at Crufts in 1957 at the age of ten. Ch. Lochinvar sired fourteen English Champions, fifteen different CC winners, plus twenty-four overseas Champions. Many of today's modern Collies trace their history back to the Ladyparks. In 1959 Miss Grey was involved in a terrible car crash and she had to spend the rest of her life in a wheelchair. Miss Grey continued to show her Collies with the help of her many friends, but it was the end of a fabulous era.

The Northern Collie Club, founded in 1885, was the first breed club. In the early 1900s the Collie Club and the Rough Collie Blue Merle Club came into existence. On March 21st 1923 interested members of these clubs met to discuss the amalgamation. Application was made to the Kennel Club on January 24th 1924, and a new era began with the formation of the British Collie Club. The Smooth Collie Club joined forces with the British Collie Club in 1932. The club is the proud owner of one of the most coveted trophies in the breed – the Collie Club Challenge Trophy, a truly outstanding work of art. This beautiful trophy was won by Mr Mycroft's Ch. Mywicks Meadow

Int. Ch. Lochinvar of Ladypark: Best of Breed at Crufts in 1951 and 1957, sire of fourteen English Champions.

Pictured left to right: Westcarrs Blue Michael, a son of Ch. Westcarrs Blue Minoru, Geoffdens Imagination and Westcarrs Whacko.

Lancer in 1957, 1959 and 1961. Another well-known breeder to take this trophy home three times was Mr Tom Purvis, who won it in 1977 and 1978 with Ch. Danvis Ladyvale Blue Mist, and then in 1979 with Ch. Danvis Ladyvale Blue Macade, a full brother to Blue Mist. In 1966 the Collie Breed Council was formed to further the interests of the Rough and Smooth Collie. This Breed Council still exists today, and does an excellent job for the breed in general.

In the 1930s a young Scotsman dreamt of owning a Collie. Eventually he contacted Mr Lord of the Seedley Collies, who quoted him the price of £11 for a pup. His father told him to put the idea out of his head, and it was not until 1943, when he was just married, that his dream of owning a Rough Collie came true. The man was Harry P. McLaren, and this was the start of the famous Narragansette Collies. Mr McLaren bought a puppy from a Mrs James of Blantford, and this Collie pup was called Laird. Although this dog was not suitable for the show ring, he was a most wonderful companion and lived with the McLarens all his life. The second puppy was chosen with exhibiting in mind, and this was a bitch, called Vanity, obtained from Miss Grey of the Ladypark prefix. Mr McLaren started breeding Collies in his own right in 1947, and soon his reputation

Harry McLaren, pictured with Ch. Forth of Narragansette in 1953.

Ch. Snowgarth of Narragansette, one of the many Champions to come from Harry McLaren's kennels.

grew and his dogs were exported to many countries, particularly to America. Today Harry McLaren is still to be seen in the ring as an exhibitor, and he is much sought after as an International Championship judge. He has judged Crufts twice and also awards CCs in Smooth Collies.

The Jefsfire kennels, owned by Alan and Kath Jeffries, is one of Britain's leading kennels and has been breeding top winning exhibits for over forty years. The foundation bitch was of Whitelea breeding, and she was mated to Ch. Loyal of Ladypark. In the resulting litter was Jefsfire By Achievement; he was not a good showman, but he made up for it by siring Ch. Jefsfire Amberlinnet in a litter out of Whitelea Watastra. Jefsfire Satin Sensation was mated to Ch. Gunner of Glenturret and produced the famous dog, Ch. Jefsfire Strollaway. He was only at stud for a limited period, but he produced some outstanding Rough Collies.

Mr Jeffries recalls his early days in the breed, and in particular, an incident relating to George Archer of the Whitelea Collies, known in those days as the 'likeable rogue' in the Midlands. Apparently a lady from Birmingham had booked her bitch to Ch. Leonartes of Ladypark, who was

Ch. Jefsfire Strollaway, born in 1958, sire of many Champions.

Ch. Mywicks Satine A Simba Star: holder of the Rough Collie Bitch CC record with sixteen CCs.

Ch. Pattingham Pacemaker: the first Rough Collie to win a Working Group at Crufts, 1964.

owned by George Archer. Unfortunately the bitch was ready to be mated on a Sunday, and the young lady had to miss her weekly church visit to be at Derby by 10. 30a.m. on her arrival she was dismayed to find that the well-known breeder lived in a run-down villa-type house. However, visitors were always made very welcome by George and his mother, and after some refreshment, they went out to supervise the mating in the small backyard, which was completely surrounded by back-to-back houses. The mating took place, much to the embarrassment of the young lady, who noticed that every upstairs window overlooking the yard was filled with spectators. "Don't the neighbours complain?" she asked Mr Archer. "No", he replied. "If they did, I would not let them stay." It transpired that Mr Archer owned the whole row of houses!

The Jeffries' kennel continues to go from strength to strength, and one of their recent Champions made history by winning his title in just three weeks. The sable dog, Ch. Lasheen Stolen Property

Ch. Kesbury Coquette. owned by Mrs R. Cozens.

from Jefsfire, was a consistent winner from the word go, taking many Best Puppy awards, and winning his title at a very early age. The Rough Collie is now so popular that I cannot hope to mention all the top kennels, but over the last thirty years some outstanding Collies have been bred and exhibited by a number of experienced breeders, who have truly cared about the welfare of their breed. Mrs Margaret Franklin of the Pattingham prefix has bred some outstanding dogs, including the very handsome dog Ch. Pattingham Pacemaker. He had the most beautiful colour coat, a deep-shaded dark mahogany sable, set off by a huge white collar – what a magnificent sight he was! Geoff Mildon, a great character in the breed – always recognised by the special hat he wore in the ring – made an impact with his Geoffdon Collies.

Frank Mitchell bred the lovely Glenmist Collies, including Ch. Sapphire of Glenmist, and the sisters Ch. Lovely Lady of Glenmist and Ch. Pattinghan Gay Lady of Glenmist. Gay Lady was the dam of Ch. Pattingham Pacemaker. Frank Mitchell was also the name behind Ch. Debonair of Glenmist, Golden Legacy of Glenmist, Ch. Spellbinder of Glenmist and many more outstanding Collies.

Mrs Floss Chapman of the Deloraine Collies bred a number of Champions, including: Ch. Deloraine Distinctive, Ch. Deloraine Decorative, Ch. Deloraine Dinamite, Ch. Deloraine Don Juan, and many other CC winners. In fact, I purchased my lovely Deloraine Dilemma from Mrs Chapman back in 1967, and every Collie I have bred goes back to her, including my Smooth Collies.

John Parrot has produced some beautiful golden sable colours in his Larkena Rough Collies. Ch. Larkena Vanara Golden Victor and the heavy-coated Ch. Larkena Rabelais were well used as stud dogs, and they are both behind many of today's top winners. Mywicks Meadow Lancer sired thirteen Champions, including the fantastic tricolour bitch Ch. Satine of Simbastar, who won fifteen CCs. He also sired Ch. Duntiblae Dog Watch for Diane Cochrane, who had a very successful kennel of Rough Collies, including Ch. Duntiblae Dog Star and Ch. Duntiblae Dingo.

Pelido Rough Collies – Champions in three different colours. Pictured (left to right): Ch. Jeffield Esquire, Ch. Pelido Black Belle, Ch. Cathenbrae Polar Moon at Pelido, Ch. Pelido Sparticus, Ch. Pelido Angel Fingers, Ch. Pelido Silver Lady and Ch. Jaden Mister Blue at Pelido.

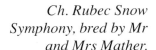

Ch. Rubec Snow Symphony, bred by Mr and Mrs Mather.

To bring the Rough Collie scene up to the present day, mention should be made of the Bhyllsacre kennels, owned by Mrs R. Cozens. She has enjoyed considerable success in the show ring and has also produced some first-class stock, including the beautiful bitch Ch. Bhyllsacre Querida Mia and more recently, Ch. Kesbury Coquette. The Drenoss kennel, owned by mother and daughter Roz and Denise Cartwright, is also making a name for itself. In 1992 Ch. Easy Come at Drenoss was winning well, plus a super young sable dog, Drenoss I Wanna Be Famous – and I am sure he will be! Mr and Mrs Anderton bred the fabulous Ch. Karava Kornishman, a superb tricolour dog, not only performing well in the ring but also as a sire. He has put his mark on many of today's top winners.

Three generations of Ingledene breeding. Pictured (left to right): Ch. Ingledene Summer Love, Ch. Ingledene First Love, and Ingledene Cherish the Love.

Some kennels are more productive than others, for not everyone can keep a team of stud dogs. However, Lisa and Peter Burtenshaw are noted for keeping a team of top winning stud dogs, in all three colours. I visited their kennels when I went to use one of their dogs, Ch. Cathenbrae Polar Moon at Pelido, on my Smooth bitch, Ch. Dancerwood Bewitched at Astrellita, and I was very impressed by the way that all the Pelido dogs were kept in the most immaculate condition, and every one of them was dearly loved. Many top winners have come from the Pelido kennels, not only in the UK but also overseas. Most breeders can only afford to keep a few select bitches, and so careful study of pedigrees is essential in order to line-breed to sound stock. In this way a small kennel can still produce as many Champions as the bigger kennels. One example of this is the Rubec kennels, owned by Mr and Mrs Mather from Co. Durham, who were top breeders for 1989, owning Ch. Rubec Blue Peter and breeding that lovely blue bitch, Ch. Rubec Snow Symphony.

The Ingledene kennels owned by Mr and Mrs Val Geddes were originally based in Ireland, but in recent years they have made their home in Wales where they have bred some super stock, most particularly Ch. Ingledene First Love, who won a Champion Stakes class beating 200 other Champions. Sometimes a kennel is not as lucky as it deserves to be, and Ken Greenhalgh's Edgemont Katarina, a truly lovely tricolour bitch, was very unlucky not to gain her title. In my opinion, she was more than worthy of her crown, with her stand-off aloofness and elegance, not often seen these days. Her arched neck and lovely body shape were a great pleasure to see.

The Rifflesea kennels stand out as just about the most famous of the Rough Collie kennels, with

Ch. Rifflesea Romantasy.

Ch. Rose of Ladypark and Ch. Lad of Ladypark: this pair were bred together three times and produced a Champion in each litter.

a history that goes back some fifty years. Hazel Hunt (now Collin) decided when she was very young that the Rough Collie was to be her breed. Her first Collie was purchased in 1943 from Mrs Nadine George of the Beulah Collies. The puppy, Beulahs Golden Fantasy, cost twelve guineas of hard-earned money, and was sired by Ch. Beulahs Golden Future out of Ch. Beulahs Golden Feather. There were no Championship shows during the war years and showing was restricted, but the bitch enjoyed a few modest wins at local shows. It was at one of these shows that a young medical student, who was hoping to buy a Rough Collie, was introduced to Hazel Hunt. Not only did Hazel succeed in getting him a Rough Collie from the famous Ladypark kennels, she also ended up by marrying him! The dog was to become Ch. Lad of Ladypark, and he was the first Ladypark Collie to win a CC – and so the stage was set.

From wedding present money, they purchased a bitch puppy sired by Lad's full brother, Ch. Lochinvar, and what an investment that turned out to be! This was Lochinvar's first litter and it included three future Champions. Hazel's bitch was Ch. Rose of Ladypark, who went to her first Championship Show at eight months and won Best Puppy and the Reserve CC. As a puppy, she was never beaten, winning two CCs, and then she won her title at her first show as an adult. Ch. Rose was bred to Ch. Lad three times, and she produced a Champion in each litter. Meanwhile Hazel's first bitch, Beulahs Golden Fantasy, produced just one surviving puppy – a blue merle, named Lilac of Ladypark – and it was this bitch who was to start the lovely coloured merles that made Margaret Osborn's name. In a subsequent litter Beulahs Golden Fantasy produced a tricolour dog, Rifflesea Royalist. He carried very little white on him – he was almost black and tan – but he sired the great Ch. Westcarrs Blue Minoru, Westcarrs Blue Mine (winner of two CCs), the lovely Ch. Lovely Lady of Glenmist and her sister Ch. Pattingham Gay Lady at Glenmist, in only four litters.

Miss May Young and her sister, well-known for their Ugony prefix, became very interested in the Rough Collie at this time. They purchased a daughter of Alphington Landgirl, who was then mated to Ch. Lad of Ladypark, and she produced five puppies. Hazel had the pick of the litter and she chose a golden sable dog with a huge shawl collar, who was to become the beautiful Ch. Ugony's Golden Son O Lad at Rifflesea. He was shown by Miss May Young and won many top awards, including runner-up to Best in Show at the Three Counties Championship Show. Over the years Hazel has had the pleasure of making up many Champions and they include: Ch. Lad of Ladypark, Ch. Rose of Ladypark, Ch. Rifflesea Resplendence, Int. Ch. Rifflesea Regality of Dunsinane, Ch. Rifflesea Reward of Glenmist CD, Ch. Ugony's Golden Son O Lad of Rifflesea, Ch. Rifflesea Reminds Me of Blue Mist at Bleckhill, made up in 1992, as was Ch. Rifflesea Romantasy, who won her title at the National Working Breeds under the well-known judge and breeder, Mrs Lyn Westby.

On a judging trip to Italy, Hazel was very impressed with a young, beautifully marked, blue merle dog, Int. Ch. Incredibly Blu di Cambiano and she awarded him Best in Show. After the show she approached the owner, Mrs Garabelli, to chat about the dog's virtues, and this resulted in Mrs Garabelli sending the dog to England for a year, so that Hazel could campaign him to his English title, and offer him at stud to English Collie breeders. Incredibly Blu quickly gained his English title, along with the Pedigree Chum/Our Dogs trophy for top sire in the breed – the first time this award had gone to a blue merle. This lovely blue dog sired nine Champions in five different countries, and when he left England he went on to Sweden – a truly remarkable dog.

Mr and Mrs Hickson of the Bririch Collies, have produced some top-quality blue merles, including the handsome Ch. Blue Rock of Bririch, who produced Ch. Bririch Blue Unit, Ch. Mossylea Moody Blue and Ch. Ingledene Blue Rain. The Hicksons' bitch, Ch. Bririch Blue Yvette

Ch. Antoc Midnight Cowboy: winner of the Pedigree Chum Veteran Stakes three years in succession.

produced Ch. Bririch Blue Ripple. The top winning blue merle of 1992 is Angela Hodgson's Ch. Tamelia Gordon Bennet, a son of Ch. Upperton Blue Brand out of a daughter of Int. Ch. Incredibly Blu di Cambiano.

In 1964 Mr and Mrs Eglin took a young tricolour bitch, Witchraft of Rokeby (later to become a Champion), to Mrs Audrey Chatfield's well-known Dazzler of Dunsinane, and from this litter came three Champions: Ch. Royal Ace of Rokeby, Ch. Romney of Rokeby and Ch. Rosemarie of Rokeby – three outstanding Rough Collies. Ch. Romney was mated back to her own sire (Dazzler) and produced the fantastic Ch. Ramsey of Rokeby, and Ch. Rosalinda of Rokeby. This was the beginning of the famous Rokeby kennels. Since then Champion after Champion has been produced. I remember going to the Rokeby kennels to use Ch. Ramsey on one of my bitches, and I was allowed to see all their Collies, which was deemed to be a great honour. I had the privilege of seeing over forty magnificent Collies – a sight to remember. Ramsey had the most beautiful expression you could ever wish to see, and he passed this on to all his offspring.

Mrs Chatfield of the Dunsinane kennel. has done so much to promote the breed with her *International Handbook*, produced every year in time for Crufts. This book is eagerly awaited, and is a sort of Collie bible in pictures, as Collie lovers worldwide use the book to advertise their stock. Mrs Chatfield has judged throughout the world, and although she does not breed any longer, the Dunsinane blood runs through almost every Collie since the early fifties. Dogs such as Ch. Dorgano, Ch. Defender, Ch. Deborah and Ch. Darling (of Dunsinane) all made their mark.

When I first came into the breed in 1967 I was very impressed with Mrs Aileen Speding's Antoc Collies, who were winning well in the ring. I took one of my bitches to be mated to the very handsome Ch. Antoc Vicar of Bray. I was made very welcome and I stayed for tea in Mrs Speding's lovely beamed cottage. It was while I was sitting there that I made up my mind that one day I would have a beamed cottage with Collies all around me, just like Mrs Speding, and as I write this book I am sitting in my own beamed cottage with Collies, Rough and Smooth all around me! Mrs Speding's Antoc Collies trace back to the Eden kennels and the Ladypark Kennels. Ch. Antoc Vicar of Bray's pedigree can be traced through his dam, Antoc Rosemarie, who was a

Ch. Lowerpark Izafella, bred by Lyn Westby. One of the many Champions to come from this kennel.

daughter of Antoc Tawny Lyric; Lyric was a daughter of Antoc Tawny Token, and Token was a daughter of Ch. Ugonys Golden Son O Lad of Rifflesea. Ch Antoc the Boyfriend was a son of Ch. Antoc Daydream; and Ch. Antoc Midnight Cowboy was a son of Antoc Griffin – all in all very impressive breeding. The tricolour, Midnight Cowboy, was the winner of many CCs and held the title of winner of the Pedigree Chum veteran stakes class for three years in succession. A favourite of mine is Ch. Antoc April Love, who has done a lot winning, including Reserve Best of Group at Crufts.

Another kennel that I was impressed by in my early days in the breed was the Lowerpark kennels, owned by Mrs Lyn Westby, who has been breeding Rough Collies since 1950, starting with Beulahs and Eden bloodlines. The Eden bitch mated to Ch. Westcarrs Blue Minoru produced a Swedish Champion in her first litter, and in a direct line from her came Ch. Lowerpark Blue Cloud of Glenmist, Ch. Lowerpark Black Buccaneer, Ch. Lowerpark Izafella and Ch. Lowerpark Star Spangled, as well as many other CC winning Collies. Ch. Black Buccaneer produced CC winners in all three colours, and he is behind many of the blue bred dogs of today. Lyn also bred the well-known Ch. Lowerpark Moonlighter at Corydon, owned by John and Barbara Blake, who have shown him to many top awards. He gained his title from just five shows in six weeks.

John and Barbara have been in Collies for many years. Barbara started with her first show dog, a grandson of Ch. Lochinvar of Ladypark, in 1956. In fact, Barbara was brought up with Collies, as her grandfather kept and showed the breed from 1910 to 1950. Barbara met John at a dog show where John was showing his own first Collie, Light Cavalry of Ladypark, and they married in 1960. The couple then set about breeding some of the country's finest Rough Collies. They purchased a bitch called Chuckalucks That's My Girl and mated her to Ch. Jefsfire Strollaway on two occasions. In the first litter she produced Corydon Bella Donna, and the second litter included the sisters Corydon Isa Bella, winner of two Reserve CCs, and Corydon Cara Bell, who was the kennel's first Junior Warrant winner. Bella Donna was mated to the leading sire of the day, Ch. Larkena Vanara Golden Victor, and she produced the Reserve CC winning Corydon Vicisti. He, in turn, was mated to Corydon Coal Black Maid, who was a daughter of Ralvera's Donnasmaid, and

Ch. Aust. Ch. Corydon Tucks Tiger, now living in Australia. The Corydon kennel has produced fourteen English Champions and nineteen overseas Champions.

from the resulting litter came the outstanding tricolour dog, Corydon Quo Vadis.

At this time a new purchase joined the kennel in the form of Regality of Rokeby. She was royally bred from the brother and sister mating of Ch. Royal Ace of Rokeby and Ch. Romney of Rokeby, and she was to prove a great asset to the kennels. When she was mated to Quo Vadis, she produced Corydon Qui Vive, a beautiful sable bitch, who is behind almost all of the Corydon Collies. In a later litter Regality was mated to her parents' full brother, Royal Flush of Rokeby, and this time she produced Corydon King Hector, a fine upstanding sable dog. By mating half-brother to half-sister (Qui Vive to King Hector) the kennels' first Champion was produced – the lovely bitch Ch. Corydon Hippolyta – fifteen years and six generations from That's My Girl.

Qui Vive gained her title in 1975, and she was mated to Ch. Ramsey of Rokeby to produce that lovely tricolour dog, Ch. Corydon Quinault, who went on to become an Australian Champion. He, in turn, produced two Champion sons, Ch. Corydon Handsome Hero and Ch. Little Caesar at Corydon, both born in 1977. When Little Caesar went off to Australia it was a sad day for the UK as he could have done so much for the breed here. However, he left four British Champions, so all was not lost. Among his Champion offspring was Ch. Corydon Handsome Hotspur. I judged this dog and found him to be one of the soundest movers on the day, and I awarded him his third CC. Another sound moving dog was the tricolour Ch. Corydon Tucks Tiger, who won his title and a Reserve Group at a Championship Show in the UK before leaving for Australia. In his new home he quickly gained his title, winning sixteen CCs, all with Best of Breed, in an unbeaten run which included nine Groups and seven Best in Shows (all-breeds Championship Shows). Before Tiger left the UK he sired the top winning blue merle dog Ch. Lowerpark Moonlighter at Corydon, who to date has won eleven CCs. The Corydon kennel has a record to be proud of, and in the last thirty years careful line breeding has produced fourteen English Champions and nineteen overseas Champions.

Chapter Three

SMOOTH COLLIE HISTORY

Smooth Collie classes were held as early as 1877, and one of the earliest fanciers was a Mr Hastie who lived in Newcastle and owned the Herdwick prefix. He was soon followed by many famous names, and as the breed gained in popularity, the hard work of many well-known breeders brought about the lovely, regal Smooth Collie as we know it today. In 1917 the tricolour Smooth Collie, Ch. Laund Lynne, was born. She was bred by Mr Whitley and owned by Mr W. Stansfield, whose Laund prefix was known all over the world. This Smooth bitch was a legend in her day, winning seventeen CCs and ninety-five Best in Show awards. Many Collie fanciers, Rough and Smooth, will know that Mr Stansfield was the father of Mrs Ada Bishop, who has carried on the Laund prefix with many beautiful Collies.

During the First World War an injunction from the Kennel Club banned all dog breeding, and no litters could be bred except under special licence. This must have been a bitter blow as the ban lasted three years, and we remain grateful to the staunch Smooth Collie lovers, such as Mr Stansfield (Laund), Mr A. Newton (Haighton), Mr B. Hewison (Hewburn), and Rayner Anderson (Saltaire), for looking after the interests of the breed by carefully breeding and rearing Smooth Collies in such hard times. Many of these Smooth Collies carried the prefixes of Laund, Hewburn, and Haighton, and many notable Smooth Collies hit the top spots in the early thirties.

One of the nicest Smooth Collies around at this time was Ch. Black Dorcas, who was a beautiful tricolour bitch, bred by Mrs Zoe Rhys. Mrs Rhys was a real stalwart of the breed and produced many beautiful Smooth Collies. Her Hughley prefix became well-known for Roughs as well as Smooths, and she was a founder member of the London Collie Club and patron of the Smooth Collie Club of Great Britain. She purchased her first Smooth Collie in 1919, and was still going strong and exhibiting her Smooths in 1977. Her first Smooth was registered as Blue Amber, because this bitch's blue coat had a sandy-coloured tinge. In 1924 she purchased a blue merle bitch from Tom Butterworth, and she was called Blue Orchid. She was sired by Alec Allslop's tricolour dog Black Blend, and she went on to be the dam of Ch. Blue Domino and her litter sister Oyster Lass, who was, in turn, the dam of Ch. Black Dorcas. Dorcas's litter sister was given to Mr Allslop as a puppy, and she was named Wychelms Black Lass. She produced Ch. Wychelms Silver Maid, who was the dam of Mr Pop Farrington's first Smooth Collie.

At the start of the Second World War Mrs Rhys had over thirty Smooth Collies, which was quite a number for those days. I was very fortunate in knowing Mrs Rhys, as she was still exhibiting with her Ch. Blue Heritage at Hughley, handled by Mr Trevor Hayward. Sadly Mrs Rhys died in 1986, followed just one week later by another great Smooth Collie breeder, Mrs Kay Alexander of the famous Peterblue kennels.

Elizabeth Dundas Mouat (left) pictured with Ch. Peterblue Doran and Ada Bishop with Peterblue Arabelle.

The Peterblue kennels started in the early 1950s with Ch. Redevalley Rosita of Ladypark. This bitch was bred by Gordon Foster, who, with his father, owned the Redevalley prefix. Rosita was to become the foundation bitch for Mrs Kay Alexander and her partner, Miss Elizabeth Dundas Mouat, and from this bitch comes at least 80 per cent of the Smooth Collies shown today. The partners called her 'Gussie', and she produced six Champions in three litters. It is interesting to note that on each occasion she was mated to a Rough Collie, because at that time there were so few Smooth stud dogs available. However, she was a dominant Smooth, for in all her litters she did not produce one Rough puppy. The Peterblue kennel went on to produce some of the finest Smooth Collies, which were known all over the world, and the kennel won over one hundred CCs in the UK.

One of Ch. Redevalley Rosita's puppies was sold to Mrs Joan Hill of the well-known Selskars prefix, and she was one of the most lovely tricolour Smooth bitches ever shown. Her name was Ch. Selskars Peterblue Susan, and she could walk into any show ring today and take top awards. Mrs Joan Hill bred the sable Ch. Selskars Soldanella (some say, the first sable Champion), co-owned by Mrs Jean Taylor. Another beautiful bitch, bred by Joan, was the tricolour bitch Ch. Selskars Soldanora, who was shown by Mr and Mrs Saville. She was a prolific winner in the show ring, notching up a total of eighteen CCs.

The early sixties were dominated by the Laund, the Selskars, and the Peterblue kennels. It was at about this time that Tom Purvis, well-known for his Rough Collies, took the show scene by storm with Ch. Danvis Blue Prince, who won thirteen CCs. This dog was sired by Major of Humbledon out of Danvis Gay Suzetta. Another famous Smooth Collie shown at this time was Ch. Tilehouse Patrick, a blue merle, bred and owned by Mrs Iris Combe. He was a very impressive dog, and he won a total of seventeen CCs. In 1974 Mrs Christine Leach imported the blue merle bitch Kelbonnie Chanel Gina, from Canada. She came into quarantine in whelp, having been mated to Am. Ch. Goliath O Darjoro. Christine took great care when choosing her import, and the deciding factor to clinch the deal was Gina's extrovert temperament This bitch excelled herself, producing a superb litter of four dogs and three bitches. Miss Jo Stewart, the vet, pronounced the litter healthy,

Ch. Selskars Peterblue Susan, owned by Joan Hill.

Ch. Amberhill Dark Candy.

and the pups left the quarantine kennels at six weeks of age.

From this litter came Ralph of Talcot, owned by Mrs Jane Gent, who now lives in Australia with her well-known Talcot prefix. He went on to sire Ch. Talcot Farewell at Heronlea. Mrs Rhys took the blue merle dog from the litter, and he went on to become Ch. Blue Heritage at Hughley, Best in Show at the British Collie Show in 1976, and with ten CCs to his credit. Blue Heritage was mated to Trevor and Birgit Hayward's Ch. Jalondas Jacanapes, and she produced the outstanding litter which included Ch. Foxearth Jubilation, Ch. Foxearth Jubilant and Ch. Foxearth Jubilate, thus founding another dynasty of Smooth Collies.

Trevor and Birgit Hayward of the Foxearth kennels have bred Champions in all three colours, and this is a top kennel that produces Champion stock time and time again, not only in this country

The famous Dancerwood sable Smooth Collies, pictured (left to right): Dancerwood Gem's Cygnet, Dancerwood Sun Prince, Dancerwood Sun King and Ch. Dancerwood Freelance.   *R. J. Kenward.*

Ch. Newarp Silver Moonbeam: Best of Breed at Crufts in 1986, 1987, 1988 and 1990 and winner of thirty CCs.

Ch. Astrellita Blue Movie at Glenmist: a top winning Smooth Collie with thirty CCs.

Roy Baker.

but all over the world. They are the proud owners of the UK's top stud dog, Ch. Sylbecq Draught Guinness at Foxearth, who is a magnificent show specimen, and also a great companion. Trevor also owned Ch. Dundrennan Melody, in partnership with Derek Smith, and she was the top winning Rough Collie for 1975. She was bred by Freda Thomas (formerly Marlow). This kennel is responsible for producing top winners for others to show and enjoy, such as Geoff Duffield's lovely Ch. Foxearth Jubilant, who set the show ring alight with her superb showmanship. She won her first CC and Best of Breed at Manchester in 1978 and went on to win another nine CCs, including three times Best of Breed at Crufts. She was also a Working Group finalist under the great judge Joe Braddon.

Other beautiful dogs to come from these kennels include Ch. Foxearth Freeman, Ch. Foxearth Flourish, winner of the British Collie Club Trophy, Ch. Foxearth Tinsmith, a lovely blue merle, sired by Ch. Astrellita the Silversmith, and Ch. Foxearth Gold Fever; and at this moment they are showing an exciting youngster, Ch. Sharidon Silver Phantom at Foxearth, who gained his title while still a junior, winning the CC at Crufts at the age of fifteen months.

Judith White's beautiful sables are a sight to behold, and she is still a familiar figure around the shows with her team of Smooths. Those I particularly liked include Dancerwood Gems Cygnet, and his brother Sun King, plus Ch. Dancerwood Freelance, who was the dam of my own Ch. Dancerwood Bewitched at Astrellita. Roy Baker and Mike Vincent had one of Judith's Smooth Collies, and this was Ch. Dancerwood Crown Jewel, a sister to Bewitched. She went on to produce some lovely stock for them, including the beautiful sable bitch, Ch. Sylbecq Fleur De Lys, who was dam of Ch. Sylbecq Draught Guinness at Foxearth.

Another stable of well-known Smooths is Mrs Pat Lister's Newarp Collies. She had been having a successful run with her blue bitch, Ch. Catalanta Blue Mist, and then purchased a son of Dancerwood Dellaware from me in 1978. He became Ch. Astrellita The Gunslinger of Newarp, and he produced for her Ch. Newarp Silver Moonlight, a lovely blue merle bitch, who produced seven Champions in only two litters. One of Moonlight's offspring was the CC record holder Ch.

Three generations of Astrellita Collies (pictured left to right): Ch. Astrellita Adele, her daughter Astrellita Astrid and grandaughter Astrellita Simply The Best.

Pro Dog.

Newarp Silver Moonbeam, who was Best of Breed at Crufts in 1986, 1987 and 1988, and then again in l990.

Close on her heels is the beautiful Ch. Astrellita Blue Movie at Glenmist, winner of thirty CCs. Blue Movie is owned by Mrs Lillian Mitchell, wife of Frank Mitchell, famous for his Glenmist Rough Collies. Blue Movie is a superb show girl, and has also produced many Champion children, including: Ch. Glenmist Rough Diamond, owned by Mr Colin Dale Mills, Ch. Glenmist Blue Lodestone, Ch. Glenmist Blue Diamond at Francolls – all blue merles – and the tricolour dog Ch. Glenmist Movie Maestro, owned by Jack and Valerie Turner. Blue Movie won the CC and Best of Breed at Crufts 1991 at the age of ten, and a year later she was Best in Show at the Smooth Collie Club Championship show – Lillian and Frank could never have dreamt of such a record when they came and chose her at nine weeks old! Blue Movie is the daughter of Ch. Dancerwood Bewitched at Astrellita, who also produced Ch. Astrellita Moonstone, who worked cattle for a year before taking to the show ring to gain her title in just three weeks. Bewitched was also the dam of Eng. and Australian Ch. Astrellita Midnight Dynamo.

My own Ch. Astrellita The Silversmith was a top-quality blue merle dog, and he won Best of Breed at Crufts under Mrs Lyn Westby. Lyn is a well-known judge of Collies Rough and Smooth,

Ch. Misstoff Moriarty.

and she has now become more involved with Smooth Collies after taking over the lovely Astrellita Amie, who won the CC at Crufts in 1992 under Mrs Pat Lister. My bitch, Ch. Astrellita Adele, gained her title in 1991 and was Top Smooth of the Year at the annual awards event. In fact, an Astrellita-bred Smooth Collie has won this award for three consecutive years – 1989 Ch. Astrellita The Silversmith, 1990 Ch. Astrellita Blue Movie at Glenmist, and 1991 Ch. Astrellita Adele, who was also runner-up Top Smooth 1992, pipped at the post by Ch. Newarp Silver Moonbeam.

Mrs Isobel Griffiths' Ch. Alopex Blue Stocking won her title in 1992, and this upstanding blue bitch shows off her many virtues in the ring. Isobel has done much work for the Smooth Collie and was at one time the secretary of the Smooth Collie Club; she is the KC liaison officer, and has campaigned for the ban on Rough/Smooth matings to be postponed. We now have many enthusiasts who have become smitten by the Smooth Collie. These include Mrs Jean Taylor with her lovely sable, Ch. Crossfell Bliss, and Mr and Mrs Trundley's Treewood kennels, which have produced some super Smooth Collies including the very smart tricolour dog Ch. Treewood Black King. Among the new Champions in the breed are: Ch. Misstoff Moriarty, owned by Maria and Tony Foulston, Ch. Bothways About Time Blue, Ch. Bothways Pastel Blue, Ch. Bothways Bijou, and Ch. Norfield Magic Knight. Recent CC winners include: Foxearth Flashgun, Lassina Looks Familar and Astrellita Amie.

The secretary and the treasurer of the Smooth Collie Club of Great Britain are sisters, both sharing a love of Smooth Collies. Mrs Innes Bratley, who has been treasurer of the club for many years, first came into Smooths with a blue merle bitch, bred by Mrs Iris Combe. This was Sugar of Tilehouse, born in 1973. She gained one CC, and she was to be the foundation bitch of the Amberhill kennels. This prefix is shared by the sisters and was granted in 1970. They have campaigned Amberhill Sugar Candy, winner of one CC and nine Reserve CCs, Ch. Amberhill Candy Floss, and the tricolour Ch. Amberhill Candy's Girl.

Chapter Four

VIVE LA DIFFERENCE!

The Smooth Collie differs from the Rough Collie in many ways, not only by its general appearance, but in character as well. The Smooth Collie is a much quicker to investigate when a visitor calls, while the Roughs contemplate whether a move is really necessary. I also find the Smooth Collies noisier than the Roughs; their bark is quite different in sound, and I think this can be attributed to the hound influence. The Rough Collie will yap, while the Smooth will break out into a blood-curdling yodel – although this is only likely to happen when there is a strange noise or disturbance, late at night. Both the Rough and the Smooth Collie make excellent housedogs, but the quick-thinking Smooth, with its sharp reactions, probably has the edge.

Due to its lack of body hair, the Smooth Collie has a more refined head and the ears are carried more erect, than the Rough Collie. I find that the outline of the Smooth has that extra elegance and racey style that I find so attractive in the breed. The Smooth Collie has a more agile appearance than the Rough, and I am pleased to say that in the days of changing fashions, the Smooth Collie is still bred on strong working lines, unlike the Rough Collie, which is bred mainly as a show dog. The Smooth Collie of today is a very alert and active dog, always ready to be doing something. It thrives on a busy, active life, and that is why it makes such a good working dog, and loves competing in Agility and Obedience contests. The Rough Collie has a more reticent nature, contrasting with the Smooth Collie's extrovert and bouncy nature.

It is interesting to note the difference in the Rough and Smooth, even at birth. I always find the Smooth puppy is born strong, searching for the milk bar when still attached to the placenta, while Rough Collie puppies often have to be coaxed to suckle at birth. At two and a half weeks of age a Smooth Collie will readily take solids, and by three weeks the pups will be trying to steal from the dam's plate. In fact you can have a litter of Smooths completely weaned at five weeks and the dam back in the ring by the time the pups are fifteen weeks old – and I speak from my own experience. Ch. Adele whelped a litter of six puppies in October, and in January she won Best of Breed at the London Collie Club Show, and then went on to win Top Smooth Collie at the Smooth Collie of the Year awards in March. By contrast, a Rough Collie will be out of the ring for at least six to eight months after whelping, due to the heavier coat.

You can spot a Rough puppy in a nest of Smooths at a very early stage – almost as soon as they are dry following delivery. A Rough puppy will be soft and the coat is almost shiny, while the Smooth puppy feels harder and stronger, and the coat is almost mole-like. It feels stubbly to touch and has a faint, dusty appearance. One obvious difference is in the tails: a Rough Collie puppy has a tail that is quite fat – it is almost otter-like – while a Smooth puppy's tail is quite rat-like. By the age of four months a Rough Collie puppy will be coating up quite thickly, with strong guard hairs

The Smooth Collie has a more bouncy and extrovert character than the Rough Collie, typified by Ch. Foxearth Flourish.

Steadlyn Sheer Magic, sired by Int. N. Dk. World Ch. Show Stopper. The Rough Collie is one of the most glamorous dogs in the show ring.

Pro Dog.

A sable Rough Collie puppy, showing a beautiful soft coat.

This sable Smooth Collie pup looks ungainly, but this is an equally promising puppy.

Both have strong front, good bone, well-placed dark eyes and good muzzles. The ears of the Smooth Collie are heavier, but they are the same size as the ears of the Rough Collie – it is the lack of hair which makes then appear bigger.

along the topline. A Smooth puppy will, at this stage, have lost the soft coat, and it will feel quite harsh along the topline.

At twelve to fifteen weeks the Rough puppy has the advantage over the Smooth as they are absolutely adorable, looking soft and cuddly, with a lush, thick coat framing the face. At this stage in the game the Smooth will be most ungainly – the only thing in the Smooths' favour is that their coat is not matted with food after every meal! The ears of a Smooth tend to look rather heavy and comical, but in fact, it is only the lack of fur that makes them appear out of proportion. There is, in fact, very little difference in ear-size between the Rough and the Smooth. The lack of hair on the Smooth gives an appearance of the ear being larger and much wider at the base, and this is a feature you do not notice on the Rough Collie as there is an abundance of hair at the base of the ear. By the time a Smooth Collie is six to seven months old, the dog can be shown. However, the

Nellwoods Joyful Harmony, a very handsome sable puppy pictured at ten months of age. Note how soft the coat texture is at this age. He will lose his coat at twelve to eighteen months of age, and the new coat will be much harsher to the touch.

Pro Dog.

Rough Collie will still be growing coat and feathering on the legs. Some Rough Collie puppies are ready for showing at seven months, but most do not look their best until they are at least nine months old. The dog will have a full coat, but it will be very soft and fluffy in texture. It is then a matter of seizing the opportunity to show your dog very quickly, as by twelve to fourteen months a Rough Collie will be having the first moult and will be naked as a jay bird! The coat will take at least two months to grow in again, and the adult coat will be much harsher to the touch. The Smooth will shed some hair, but the coat will grow very quickly and no Smooth need be out of the ring for more than a couple of months.

The Rough Collie, with its beautiful coat, needs much more care and attention to be kept in show condition, and a whole week must be set aside to get your Rough Collie ready for a Championship Show. However, for the enthusiast, bathing and grooming a Rough Collie is one of life's pleasures,

The Rough Collie Astrellita Able Seaman sired two Smooth Collie Champions. Pictured (left to right): Ch. Astrellita Midnight Dynamo, Astrellita Able Seaman, Major Domo, Ch. Astrellita The Silversmith, Ch. Dancerwood Bewitched of Astrellita and Ch. Astrellita Moonstone.   *Dalton.*

and there are few things more rewarding than to see the finished Rough Collie, in all its glory, prepared for the ring. The Smooth Collie, with its short coat, is very easy to keep clean and a quick rub-down is all that is needed when it comes in from the fields.

In 1966 the Smooth Collie Club of Great Britain circulated a revised Breed Standard for the Smooth Collie to its members, breaking away for all time from the Rough Collie Standard that had been shared for many years. It was not until 1974 that this new Breed Standard was finalised and the Smooth Collie had a Breed Standard in its own right. As a consequence, the English Kennel Club proposed that after 1976 no interbreeding should take place between the Rough and the Smooth Collie. It was obvious that this would happen with the changing of the Standard, but the Smooth Collie breeders were not prepared for the sudden changes that would be required in their breeding programmes. The gene pool still consisted of closely related dogs, and it was feared that if breeding to Rough Collies was banned, it would have an adverse effect on the the development of the Smooth Collie. An appeal was made to the Kennel Club, and it was agreed inter-breeding could take place in some circumstances, and, providing that permission was sought prior to the mating, they would give special dispensations.

In 1986 the Kennel Club revised all its Breed Standards so that they would conform with each other in terms of headings and terminology. It was at this point that it was stipulated that Smooth Collie breeders had only until 1993 to increase the gene pool. At this date all interbreeding ceased, and the Kennel Club will no longer register any puppies from Rough/Smooth matings. The gene pool for Smooth Collies is already very small, and this weakens any breed, as much in-breeding takes place. When breeding becomes closely related, the offspring must inevitably suffer. Ada Bishop of the well-known Laund kennels, whose family have been involved with Smooth Collies since the early l900s, spoke out against the ban, and in her book, *All About the Collie*, she states that the Smooth Collie will suffer and in time may even become extinct.

There are some Smooth breeders who welcome the ban, believing the Smooth Collie coat will improve and that the character of the Smooth Collie will be safeguarded – but what good is a coat without a body? I fear that this ban will result in a steady decline in the quality of the Smooth Collie. This will not be apparent at first, but without the influx of new blood it is certain to happen. I have used Rough blood on my Smooth bitches, and I have still managed to breed Smooth Collies that look and act like the working dog should – many of my Smooths work cattle in Britain and overseas. When I have planned Rough/Smooth matings this has been in order to improve the qualities of the Smooth, selecting for improvement of correct ears and soft, kind expression. All my Smooths have a harsh dense coat, which is waterproof and harsh to the touch. In fact, I have judged Smooths that have no Rough blood and have found a coat so smooth as to have hardly any undercoat.

From the early 1800s Rough and Smooth have been mated successfully, and kennels such as the Launds and Peterblues produced outstanding dogs. In all these years the Smooth Collie's nature has not been spoiled; they can still do a day's work when requested. I foresee Smooth Collies with poor head type, pricked ears or ears that are very low set, round eyes lacking expression, and shallow Whippet-type bodies. I hope I am proved wrong, and I hope sensible breeders will cull stock that is not correct – and cull they must, or we will have Smooth Collies with much white about the face and body, as even today quite a few Smooths carry a white factor gene. I fear that the influence of the many dedicated Smooth Collie breeders, who have worked to produce stock that is worthy of competing on equal terms with the glamorous Rough Collie, will slowly decline, and in time I am sure we will have to go back to the Kennel Club and seek permission to bring in some fresh blood.

Another factor worth considering is that with interbreeding you may have the odd Rough puppy in a litter, which is easy to sell as a pet with no papers, and this helps to pay for the Smooths you are running on. One of the problems that Smooth Collie enthusiasts face is that the public very rarely see a Smooth Collie, and so the demand for puppies is limited – if only the *Lassie* films had used a Smooth Collie! I believe that Smooth Collie breeders should make a point of showing off their stock – walking them in the park, and entering them for Agility and Obedience competitions – and in this way the public will see more of the breed and they may realise what they are missing.

Hopefully most breeders will have planned for the future and used Roughs in their mating programmes before the ban. It is vital that as many males are kept as possible, even if they go to pet homes or are kept as farm dogs, so long as the bloodlines are kept alive. Of course, the odd Rough Collie puppy may appear in future litters, and these will not be allowed to be registered at the Kennel Club, but this is a small price to pay to keep the Smooth Collie as we know it today.

Rough Collie puppies are very appealing, but you must think carefully before taking on the responsibilities of owning a dog.   *Pro Dog.*

Chapter Five

CHOOSING A PUPPY

The Collie has so much to offer as a breed and the potential owner has so much to choose from – Rough or Smooth, blue merle, sable or tricolour – plus the more obvious choices of male or female, or whether you want the Collie as a companion dog or a show dog... In all cases, the owner must first decide if a Collie will suit the particular lifestyle that is on offer. A Collie needs an interesting, stimulating life, with plenty of exercise, and human companionship. Weigh up the pros and the cons of owning the breed – a Rough Collie will moult at least once a year, leaving long hair on your carpets; a Smooth Collie will moult once a year, leaving short, sharp hairs on your carpet. Do you wish for a puppy, or maybe you would prefer an older dog? Many older Collies, Rough or Smooth, settle down in a family quite well; but having said that, there is nothing nicer than bringing home your own puppy to train and love, particularly if you have a young family, as you will be bringing up children and puppy together, thus forming a lasting bond between dog and family.

When you are ready to purchase your Collie, go along to a few dog shows with classes for Collies on offer. If possible, attend some Championship shows so that you see a variety of Rough and Smooth Collies. When you have seen a type of Collie you like, wait until after the judging and then go and see the breeders. Tell them that you have admired their dogs in the ring and you would like to visit their kennels with a view to buying a puppy.

THE COMPANION COLLIE
When you are going to choose your puppy, do be fair and say whether you want your Collie as a companion dog or as a potential show dog. Many a handsome dog has been lost to the show ring because purchasers have not been completely honest with the breeder. Equally, it is most unwise to say that you want a pet, hoping that you might get a show dog at a cheaper price. This is most unfair to the breeder who has an established reputation, and who has sold a pet puppy in good faith.

Choosing a Collie as a companion is just as important a decision as choosing for the show ring, except for the finer show points. The first thing to look for in a Collie, Rough or Smooth, is a puppy that has a happy nature and comes when called. Never take the one hiding under the chair – that dog will always be shy. Hopefully, you are going to spend the next twelve years of your life with this dog, so choose with care. Make sure that the puppy is clean; the eyes should be clear and bright, and the coat should be shiny and nice to touch. It is important that you see all members of the litter so that you can compare size and quality. You should also ask to see the dam of the litter. If the sire does not live on the premises, ask if you can see a photograph, so that you can get a rough idea of what your puppy will grow up to look like. Choose a puppy that has good bone and substance – your family will want a strong dog for long walks and games of football in the park.

MALE OR FEMALE?
I find both sexes make super family pets: they are lovable companions and will be devoted to their family. However, the majority of pet owners prefer a bitch puppy. This is something I am always surprised at, as few owners plan to use their pet for breeding. A fine, upstanding male Collie, Rough or Smooth, would always be my choice, and you do not have the problem of coping with seasons. A bitch will come into season at least once or twice a year, and this could mean dogs hanging round your gate if you have walked your bitch while she in season. Dogs have a great sense of smell and this could be a problem. If the bitch is to be a pet, and you have no plans to breed from her, it is advisable to have her spayed on her second season. If you are going to have a male puppy, you must check that the puppy is entire, i.e. that he has two testicles descended into the scrotum. If the Collie has only one testicle, this could be a problem later, as the retained testicle can become cancerous and therefore it must be removed at a suitable age, usually at around six months.

THE SHOW COLLIE
Choosing a Collie puppy for the show ring is not the easiest task, and this applies equally to the Rough and the Smooth Collie. Obviously, there are certain points to bear in mind which apply to both breeds, and indeed to all puppies of all breeds. If you have bred the litter yourself, you will know all the puppies as individuals by the time they are eight weeks old, and this will make the task of choosing a puppy that has show potential a good deal easier. However, if you are viewing the litter for the first time, you will need to rely on help from the breeder. It is important to do your homework and find out which lines you like, and this will give you some idea of what the puppies will be like when they mature.

When you go to view a litter, the first thing you should try to assess is the general well-being of the puppies. You can always tell a wormy puppy; its coat is dry and its belly swollen; the coat has a dry, stretched look and sometimes the puppy's eyes are runny. A puppy's coat, whether it is a Rough or a Smooth Collie – or any other breed – should be soft like velvet; it is almost mole-like to the touch. The next factor to assess is temperament. When you look at the litter, try to spot the bold, extrovert type, who will come up happily to meet you. Never lean over a puppy when you are trying to assess it; this will make the puppy feel overwhelmed, it will cower and not show its true character.

If you find a puppy that you like the look of, ask the breeder if you can place the pup on a table for a more detailed examination. I look for a good shoulder placement, and I check to see that the puppy has depth of chest, giving plenty of heart room. I always look for a good tail-set, as a puppy with a good tail-set will not curl its tail over its back when it is grown up. This is a fault that I cannot forgive in Collies, as it spoils the whole balance and outline of the dog. I then move to the head; this is not easy to assess in a young puppy, but at this stage you should look for a short head that has plenty of room to pull out. Look for a good stop, a short foreface and strong underjaw. At the eight week stage, the Smooth Collie should have ears of good size; if they are small they will, without a doubt, be carried erect when the dog matures. When you are trying to assess the correct ear placement and carriage, look to see if the inside edge of the ear at its base is directly above the eye.

Eye shape is one of the most important factors to look for when choosing a puppy for the show

When choosing a puppy, first make sure that is is happy, healthy and well-fed.

One Way's Classic Case, a nicely constructed blue merle Smooth Collie pictured at five months.

ring. In order to obtain that elusive expression, the eye should slope upwards at the outer corner towards the outer corner of the ear. In order for a dog with a long muzzle and stop to have full vision, the eyes must be set obliquely and be almond-shaped. The Collie must always have dark-brown eyes, unless it is a blue merle. Collies of this colour may have blue eyes, one blue eye and one brown, or even blue-flecked eyes – the colour is unimportant as long as the expression is correct, and blue merles should not be penalised for having different-coloured eyes; it is not a fault. However, round eyes are most undesirable – they leave the dog with no expression; and eyes that are too small will give the appearance of meanness in a Collie.

The colour of the puppy should be of no special importance, except for personal preference. But on a Smooth Collie, in particular, bad markings can prove to be an adult's downfall. One black or brown leg can give an illusion of bad movement; a half-white face on tricolour or sable can give the impression that the dog has no stop, and the head appears straight through. So although colour does not play such a big part in choosing a puppy, a Collie that has good markings can be eye-catching in the ring.

If you make the right decision at this stage, then when your puppy is full-grown you will, hopefully, see an animal of great beauty that has complete overall balance and style. A good head and expression are very important, but there is no point in breeding good heads on unsound bodies. There is nothing more pleasing to the eye than seeing a good Collie moving effortlessly round the ring – and with a Smooth Collie you see every muscle moving, there is no coat to cover any defects in conformation.

CARING FOR YOUR PUPPY

HOUSE TRAINING
This is rarely a problem, as all Collies are very clean and do not wish to foul their beds. Collies raised in a kennel-and-run train themselves this way. House dogs must be trained at an early age, and if your puppy makes a mess in the house, nine times out of ten the fault is your own. All puppies need to be taken out as soon as they wake from a sleep, and after every meal. Newspaper should be left by the back door for any mistakes. As the puppy grows, move the newspaper out on to the back step and show your puppy where to go. By the time your puppy is twelve weeks old, the paper will no longer be needed.

EXERCISE
No puppies should be allowed free exercise when they are very small as they tire and lose body weight, so do not ask too much of your puppy when it is young. You will do much better if you feed it, and then put it out for a short while. Try to stay with your puppy when it is playing outside and then you can assess how it is developing. When the puppy has been out long enough, put it to bed in its warm sleeping quarters, and in this way your puppy will have a good routine and will soon know what is expected.

Obviously you cannot take your puppy further than your house and garden until the inoculation programme has been completed. However, when your pup is old enough, I find that road walking not only helps to lead-train your dog, it also builds up muscle tone and keeps the dogs in good condition. When I am judging I can always tell dogs that have been road walked, and those that are left to run on grass. A Collie that is left to run free will gallop around for a while and will then lie down. The dog that is out on a lead will walk for as long as you want. This gentle exercise, every day, slowly builds strong muscular hindquarters and strong padded feet. Road walking keeps the nails short. By walking and talking with your Collie every day, you will slowly build a relationship together that will give you both years of pleasure.

HOUSING
Collies run well together, and all my dogs live together as a family. They are good mixers, but all require individual attention. They also need their own sleeping quarters. Our Collies live in a purpose-built extension leading from my office through a half-stable door. In this way I can see them at all times. In the dog-room there are extra large tea chests, fitted with bedding, and I often find two Collies in one bed!

Collies enjoy human companionship; Collies that live among a family develop their characters to their full potential. If you keep a number of dogs, it is not always possible to have all your Collies in the house, but as long as your dogs are near the house where they can see you, they have no objections to being kennelled. All Collies love family life, and the daily bustle of a household, but if your circumstances are such that your Collie has to live in a kennel, then providing it has ample space and the freedom to move around in a good-size run, it will adapt to any lifestyle very quickly.

Regardless of housing arrangements, you should set aside some time every day to socialise with your Collies. There is nothing sadder than a Collie, Rough or Smooth, who sees only a kennel, day after day, year in and year out. I like to exercise my dogs in the early part of the day, and then again in the evening. The dogs all know my routine, and they look forward to these times of the day. I do not need to look at the clock to see if it is mealtime – my Collies let me know!

CAR JOURNEYS

It is advisable to take your puppy on short car journeys in order to get it used to travelling. Most dogs love a car ride, and all my Collies cannot wait to get into the car. If I return from a shopping trip and leave the tailgate up on my car, it is full of dogs in no time – all eagerly waiting for an outing! Some people like to fit the car with wire cages for their dogs, and I must admit they are very useful for going to the dog shows that are unbenched, as you have somewhere to put your Collie while you are busy, maybe with another in the ring. Most dogs like to travel in these cages, and they are perfectly comfortable if you use a little bedding in them.

Chapter Six

TRAINING YOUR COLLIE

Collies, Rough and Smooth, are very easy to train and are quick to learn. They are always eager to please, and once a puppy understands what is required, it will never forget the lesson. Training sessions should be fun for both you and your puppy, and they should be short to begin with, building up in length as the puppy's concentration improves. Never scold your puppy too much, as it will sulk, or become unwilling to respond to you if it is anticipating a telling-off.

BASIC OBEDIENCE
For as many people who show their dogs, there are as many who enjoy Obedience work. However, all dogs should respond to some basic commands, whether you intend to train your dog for competitive Obedience, the show ring, or simply as a well-behaved companion.

For breeders training begins as soon as the puppies are mobile, starting with paper training. This is a form of training, as you praise your puppy for using the paper instead of the floor, and the pup gets the idea of responding to your wishes. Most puppies go to their new homes at around eight or nine weeks of age, and this is when the learning process really begins. All puppies respond to voice tone, and if you praise your puppy in a soft and soothing manner, and reprimand in a firm and strong manner, the puppy will soon learn if you are pleased or not. Never shout or lose your temper with your puppy, as you will only make the pup unresponsive to you. Collies are very sensitive and respond very quickly.

The first important lesson is to teach your puppy its name. Use the name to attract the puppy's attention, and then give your command, e.g. "Buddy, come", or "Buddy, stay", etc. In this way your puppy learns its name and an easy command. Always give a little treat if your puppy instantly does as you wish, and in this way the puppy will come more readily. Another early lesson, which is most important, is for the puppy to learn to stand to be groomed. These sessions do not have to last very long – just a few minutes – and the puppy will soon learn to stand still.

As your puppy grows, more basic training can be taught, such as 'Sit', 'Stay' and 'Down'. These words could save your Collie's life in an emergency, and your dog should respond instantly to each of the commands. The key to training, whether it be for show or work, is for the owner to have complete control; once you have this everything else falls into place. All Collies are very responsive and easy to train. Once you have done your own basic training, the next stage is to find a local club where you can go on to train your puppy for further show or Obedience work.

LEAD TRAINING
Never use a choke chain on your puppy. A Collie, Rough or Smooth, hates the sound of a heavy

chain around the neck. It may may be suitable for German Shepherd Dogs and Dobermans, but not for the sensitive Collie. I always use a rolled leather collar, as this is soft and does not rub away the Collie's neck coat. The next step is to attach a lead and let your puppy walk where it wants to. Do not jerk on the lead, or drag your puppy along. Let the pup get used to the lead before imposing your own wishes. A little gentle coaxing is all that is needed to get your puppy to follow you – a little piece of cheese or crispy bacon rind is usually irresistible.

As the training progresses, take the lead and gently give the command 'Come', using your puppy's name. If the pup responds, give lots of praise. If the pup fails to come, do not be angry. Call the pup again, by name, and coax with a little titbit. As soon as the puppy comes on command you should be lavish in your praise. At this stage most puppies have a habit of jumping up to you. This is a habit you must stop while the puppy is still young, as it could become a problem when the dog becomes full size. Each time the Collie jumps up, put your knee out as the dog jumps, and this will cause the dog to jump back and away from you. If you do this every time, your Collie will soon learn. All Collies want to please, and it is amazing how quickly most puppies learn. Ten minutes a day is really all that is needed, and you and your Collie should both look forward to these sessions.

TRAINING FOR THE SHOW RING

If you are planning to show your Collie it is a good idea to attend ring-training classes (ringcraft), which will help both you and your puppy to find out about what is required in the ring. No matter how beautiful your Collie is, you must train your dog for the show ring. This training is just as important as basic training, and it will give you an edge over handlers with untrained dogs, as all judges like their winners to be on their best behaviour. You cannot send an unruly dog into the Best in Show arena. Some super Collies have been unplaced because they have not co-operated for the judge's assessment. So when you enter your Collie for a show, make sure that your dog is ready not only in terms of physical appearance, but is also trained to behave correctly.

Show training should start as soon as your puppy has settled into its new home. This begins by establishing a happy relationship between you and your puppy. Handle your Collie as often as possible, brush your puppy, and handle the head, the mouth and examine the teeth as if you were a judge, so that your dog gets used to the routine. Your Collie should also get used to standing in a show stance for a few minutes at a time. Remember to praise your puppy all the time. You can make your Collie look alert and use its ears by offering a little titbit or rustling a paper bag. When you are training your puppy, I think it is essential to keep a tasty titbit in your pocket, something that is not offered at mealtimes such as bacon rind or cheese, and your Collie will soon learn that this means show training and will perform all the better. I find most dogs love cooked liver. Some dogs can be made to look alert by using a squeaky toy, but I dislike them as the noise distracts other dogs in the ring, and this obviously upsets the other handlers.

The next stage is to move your Collie on a loose lead. The dog should be moved on the lefthand side and should not be allowed to pull. If your dog pulls forward, or to the side, or breaks stride, gently jerk back on the lead, and give praise when the dog is in the correct position. You should go through this routine every day, and soon you will have a ring-perfect dog. Keep the sessions short and interesting, and reward with a titbit. As you progress, you can start to move your dog at a speed that suits you both, and that enhances the dog's movement. I find that if you move with little steps, the dog will also do little steps, giving an uneven movement. However, if you stride out, the dog will move with drive and purpose, which no dog can do if restrained too firmly. Keep the lead loose, if possible, and when you come to the end of the ring allow the Collie room to turn easily,

*Stella Clark
handling Ch.
Astrellita Adele to
look her best for
judge Joyce
Collis.*

and then guide the dog back to your side. Continue back to the starting point, and finish with your Collie standing four-square. At this point, touch your pocket – your Collie knows this is where you keep the titbits, and will therefore respond by bringing up its ears in an alert manner, giving an overall picture of poise and beauty.

As the training progresses, take your puppy to a few small shows, so that both of you get used to the atmosphere, and the puppy is not frightened of being among lots of dogs and lots of people. This will also give you the chance to compare the quality of your dog with others in the breed, and you may pick up some useful advice from other exhibitors. If you enjoy the show ring, and your Collie seems to have the makings of a successful show dog, this is the start of a whole new way of life. However, if this is not the case, you still have your Collie as a wonderful companion. If you really want to get involved with the show world you will have learned a lot, and next time you can buy a puppy that has show potential.

The first big show you attend with your Collie is a very important event in both your lives. You want to make an impact, as first impressions remain in people's minds. If your puppy is not behaving well or is not in sparkling form, you can rest assured that a poor performance will be remembered.

Chapter Seven

COLOURS OF THE COLLIE

The Collie, Rough and Smooth, comes in three colours: tricolour, blue merle, and sable and white. In America and Canada white-coloured Collies are permitted in the Breed Standard; but this colour is not permitted in the UK. All Collies should carry the typical Collie colour pattern of white legs, white feet, white mane, and a white tip to the tail. It is very rare to see a white blaze on a Rough Collie – I have not seen one for years – yet nearly all Smooths have a little white about the head, even if it is only a few hairs on the skull. Many Smooths also have a white blaze on the muzzle.

Although the same three colours apply to the Rough and the Smooth Collie, there is a marked difference in depth of colour between the two breeds. In the sable and white, for example, it is very rare to see a very dark-shaded sable Smooth Collie, or a very pale straw-like colour, whereas Rough Collies are more dominant in these colours than in any other. When it comes to tricolours, the Smooth has an edge over the Rough as almost all Smooth tricolours carry a pure black coat, with no ginger undercoat. This coat can look outstanding when it is polished up with a silk scarf. Sable and white is the most popular colour in the Rough Collie fraternity, although blue merle is now coming to the fore.

It is important to remember when judging Collies, Rough or Smooth, the dog is more important than the colour, except in the case of blue merles when dog and colour must be of outstanding quality.

THE COLLIE COLOURS AND HOW THEY WORK
Dominant sable mated to dominant sable will produce 100 per cent dominant sable.
Dominant sable mated to recessive sable will produce 50 per cent dominant sable and 50 per cent recessive sable.
Recessive sable mated to recessive sable will produce 50 per cent recessive sable, 25 per cent dominant sable, and 25 per cent tricolour.
Dominant sable mated to tricolour will produce 100 per cent recessive sable.
Recessive sable mated to tricolour will produce 50 per cent recessive sable and 50 per cent tricolour.
Tricolour mated to tricolour will only ever produce tricolour.
Tricolour mated to sable will produce tricolour and sable. (An entire litters of tricolours may be produced if the sable is recessive sable.)
Tricolour mated to blue merle will produce tricolour and blue merle, but again, it can produce whole litters of tricolours.

Blue merle mated to tricolour will produce blue merle and tricolour.

Blue merle mated to blue merle will produce mainly blue merles, but has been known to produce whole litters of tricolours. The merle to merle mating can, and often does, produce defective whites.

Dominant sable mated to a blue merle will produce 50 per cent sable merle and 50 per cent recessive sable.

Recessive sable mated to blue merle produces 25 per cent recessive sable, 25 per cent sable merle, 25 per cent blue merle and 25 per cent tricolour.

Dominant sable merle mated to tricolour produces 50 per cent sable merle and 50 per cent recessive sable.

Recessive sable merle mated to tricolour produces 25 per cent recessive sable merle, 25 per cent recessive sable, 25 per cent tricolour, and 25 per cent blue merle.

SABLE

This is the most exciting colour because there are so many shades of sable ranging from from pale straw to rich dark mahogany. The straw-like colour is highly undesirable, and it should be avoided. It is the result of always mating sable to sable, with no tricolour genes to enrich the sable. The very dark shade of mahogany is seldom seen these days, although it is permitted within the Breed Standard.

Astrellita Alicia, showing correct sable markings, perfectly balanced head, semi-erect ears and dreamy expression.

Ch. Easy Come at Drenoss: a beautiful golden sable.

It is very rare to see a a dark-shaded sable Smooth Collie – they are usually more of a golden colour – though the sable colour has never been popular in the Smooth fraternity. It is certainly more difficult to make up a sable Smooth into a Champion; I have no idea why, as I find them quite lovely. In recent years a few sable Smooths have gained their titles, but this has been the result of hard work and perseverance by their owners – even though they were beautiful specimens.

Sable is dominant over all colours. If you want a sable litter and you have a tricolour bitch, you will produce an all sable litter if the bitch is mated to a dominant sable dog. In Rough Collies, there is a wide choice of dominant sables, but in Smooths there are a very limited number of sables, let alone dominant sables. Now that Rough/Smooth matings are no longer allowed, I think there is a high risk of the sable colour disappearing from Smooth Collies. The reason for this problem is that blue merles and tricolours have become increasingly popular in the show ring over recent years, and no one has concentrated on keeping the Smooth sable gene pool up to date.

Two sables can produce tricolours. I mated two sables who had no tricolour on the pedigree until the sixth generation, and the result was nine tricolour dogs and one sable bitch (this was a recessive litter, I might add). The bitch in question was the shaded sable Astrellita Alona (a daughter of Ch. Ramsey) and she was mated to Ch. Beaublade Barrister. I kept one of these dogs, Astrellita Able Seaman, and when I used him at stud I found that when he mated a sable bitch, the majority of puppies were sable, and when he mated a blue merle bitch, the result was nearly always a litter with a majority of merles. In order to test to test if your sable is dominant, mate to a tricolour, and if all the litter are sable you will prove your point.

It is not a good idea to mate sable and white to blue merle, as although you may produce what you want in the first litter, you risk leaving a legacy of bad colour for future generations, and unsuspecting novices could well wonder why they have produced a sable with white patches, or even a sable with blue eyes. It is unfair to spoil the gene pool for the sake of one litter.

SHADED SABLE

This is a far more interesting colour than a pale sable as the coat is made up of many colours of black, gold, and even wolf colour. The colours fuse together to produce a blend of red and gold and black. It is very rare to produce this colour from pale sables, and in most instances the grandparents would be carrying the recessive tricolour gene.

Cronys Shades of Golden Light. The shaded sable becomes darker as the dog gets older.

Nellwood's Ghostbuster: This Rough Collie is a shaded sable, a colour that is confined to Rough Collies. Note the dark V on his back skull joins up with the ear colour and flows down into the white mane. Pro Dog.

TRICOLOUR

The colour tricolour is recessive. Tricolour refers to a black dog with white and tan markings. The body is black with tan on the legs and about the face. White markings should be confined to the neck and legs, and never above the back hocks. If white appeared above the hocks the dog would be termed white-factored and could not be shown. Two tricolour genes must be present to produce a tricolour; and tricolour to tricolour will only produce tricolour.

A tricolour mated to a sable will produce both sable and tricolour, unless the sable is dominant. This combination has been known to produce a whole litter of tricolours. A tricolour mated to a blue merle will produce tricolours and merles, or all tricolours, or all blue merle. The tricolour must never show a rusty tinge in the coat.

Dutch Int. Ch. Foxearth Markylla Flicka: a tricolour.

BLUE MERLE

Blue merle is one of the oldest Collie colours, and it was the most common colour seen in the early sheepdogs. However, this colour went out of fashion in the 1800s, and many blue merle puppies were culled at birth. Fortunately, a breeder called Mr W. Arkwright pioneered to make blue merles popular again towards the end of the nineteenth century, and he made a special study of how to produce the best colours. He discovered that the best blue merles were produced when tricolour was mated to blue merle, and then the blue merle offspring were mated to tricolour. Mr Arkwright went on to produce the first blue merle Champion, Ch. Blue Ruin, and in 1888 he won the Collie Trophy for Best of Breed with the first blue merle ever to win this award. From then onwards, blue merles were back in fashion. When Ch. Blue Ruin was six years old she was sold to

A group of tricolours from the Steadlyn kennels (left to right, front row): Int. N. Dk. World Ch. Show Stopper, Int. N. Dk. Ch. Steadlyn Ravishing Saga, Steadlyn Silk Mitten (eight months). (Back row): Steadlyn Sheer Magic (eight months), and Steadlyn Signature.

Pro Dog.

America, but she left some very useful stock behind to carry on her exceptional colour. In 1907 the Rough Blue Merle Collie Club was formed, and later joined forces with the Collie Club and the Northern Collie Club to become The British Collie Club. This club was later joined by the Smooth Collie Club, and it is now one of Britain's largest Collie clubs.

Blue merle is arguably the most attractive and distinctive of the Collie colours, and it is certainly the hardest colour to breed correctly. Not only do you have to breed a good specimen in terms of temperament and conformation, you are also striving for the perfect colour and markings. A blue merle coat should be predominantly clear silvery-blue, marbled with black. The Collie should also carry rich tan markings on its cheeks and eyebrows, although if the tan is not strong this fault

Int. N. Dk. It. Club Ch. Steadlyn Zong of Zweden: a beautiful blue merle, showing a silvery-blue coat and rich tan markings.

Pro Dog.

Ch. Glenmist Rough Diamond: a blue merle Smooth Collie.

Shep's Huckleberry Boy, sired by Int. N. Dk. World Ch. Show Stopper, showing a well marked blue merle head. Note the rich tan and good pigment, and dark, expressive eyes. Pro Dog.

Steadlyn Fairy Snow: Reserve World Youth Champion: a lightly marked blue merle. Pro Dog.

Steadlyn Heavenly Sent: this bitch is more heavily marked, but it does not detract from the expression. Pro Dog.

should not be penalised too severely. It is more important that the blue is really clear, and there should not be any rusty or slate markings on the body. Large black patches are considered undesirable, and excessive white – other than the usual white collar, white legs and white feet – should always be penalised, although a white blaze is allowed on all three Collie colours.

Breeding from Collies with excessive white in blue-to-blue matings is asking for trouble as they could produce defective whites – not to be confused with the white-coloured Collie. Defective white Collies stand a high risk of being blind and deaf. These defects cannot be confirmed until the puppy is six weeks old, and then it is a terrible wrench to have the dog put down. Blue to blue matings should only be carried out by very experienced breeders, and even then they can go wrong.

Blue merle is a modification of black, due to the dilution factor and due to the granules of pigmentation in each hair being less numerous than in dogs of other colours. Some of the best blue merles have come from blue merle to tricolour matings, and one of the loveliest was Ch. Astrellita Blue Movie of Glenmist. She was bred from the beautiful coloured blue dog, Ch. Cathenbrae Polar Moon at Pelido, who was a Rough Collie. His coat was the most magnificent colour, and he was pure blue-bred. He was a grandson of the beautifully marked blue Ch. Cathenbrae Willow Pattern, who was the son of Mrs T. Taylor's Ch. Cathenbrae Ladypark Lavender. He was mated to Ch. Dancerwood Bewitched of Astrellita, a tricolour of outstanding quality. She was from sable and tricolour parents, but the tricolour side of her pedigree was mostly blue-bred. The resulting litter sired by Ch. Cathenbrae Polar Moon at Pelido out of Ch. Dancerwood Bewitched of Astrellita, took the show ring by storm. The blue dog, Int. Ch. Astrellita Blue Macho went to Switzerland to work cattle and still found time to compete for his title. His sister is the great Ch. Astrellita Blue Movie at Glenmist, who has won a total of thirty CCs.

So remember blue to blue should be avoided, and sable to blue should also never be attempted as this mating will always produce rusty-coloured merles and blue-eyed sables, not always in the first litter, but these traits will lie recessive and crop up in future generations.

SABLE MERLE
Apart from the usual colours some matings, such as dominant sable to blue merle, will produce 50 per cent sable merles and 50 per recessive sables. A sable merle may be born sable, but with a bluish tinge to the coat. Sometimes this colour blue can disappear by the time the puppy is a few weeks old, but it is more likely that the puppy is left with a bluish brown tinge over the coat, which is highly undesirable, and it may have blue or blue-flecked eyes, which looks dreadful on a sable Collie.

THE WHITE COLLIE
The term 'white Collie' has two meanings. In the UK, we refer to a 'white factored' Collie, and a 'defect white', and these two types should not be mixed up or confused. The white Collie is not allowed to be registered or shown in any country, other than North America. In the US, this colour has been purposefully bred for many years, and classes are allocated for this colour at dog shows. It is becoming increasingly popular and white Collies have won Groups at major shows across the United States.

It is generally believed that white was not allowed in the original British Breed Standard because of a shepherd's traditional dislike for a white dog. A white Collie is lost among the sheep, and cannot be seen from a distance. It is also believed that sheep do not take so much notice of a white dog, and lambs will follow a white dog mistaking it for their mother. This was the only reason why

This is one of a number of white Collies owned by Queen Victoria.

Sheik du Mont, owned by Fr Linegger.

Courtesy Gerald Martin, Switzerland.

white was omitted from the Breed Standard, and not because the white Collie was in any way inferior. Breeders in England have adhered to this Standard ever since. It is believed that Queen Victoria had several white Collies. One, named Squire,was certainly white, but it is not known if he was bred from sables, so he could have been a white factored Collie, or what is known as a dilute white.

The white Collie, Rough or Smooth, is 90 to 99 per cent all white, and is homozygous in carrying both genes for the white factor. The head of the white Collie carries usual tricolour, sable, or merle colouring, and often carries a mark of the same colour on the body. The white Collie is the result of mating two Collies each carrying the white gene, meaning each parent must be white or white factored. The white Collie is not to be confused with the white factored Collie, who can be tricolour, sable or blue merle, but will be heavily marked with white, having a huge white collar often past the shoulder, excessive white on the hindlegs and over the hock and stifle.

White Collies in the UK, other than those imported from the United States, are the result of

The white Collie is popular in North America, where this colour is permitted in the Breed Standard. The white Collie is 90 to 99 per cent white, with sable, tricolour or merle colouring on the head, and often a mark of the same colour on the body.
Evelyn Mougeot.

repeatedly mating blue merle to blue merle, and not the result of white factored Collies. These mismark dogs are often termed white merle. To purposefully breed from these white merles is a very risky thing to do. It should only be undertaken by experienced breeders who are prepared to cull any or all the litter if they are born blind or deaf – some may not have any eyes at all. However, not all the resulting puppies from these matings are affected, or no one would ever try to breed on from these dogs.

A dominant merle producer from this mating, as long the dog was one hundred per cent sound, would enhance the gene pool, even though such a dog could not be shown in the UK. However, it should never be mated to another merle as this would most probably produce defective whites. There are more white factored Smooth Collies than Rough Collies in the UK, and in recent years many have turned up due to the limited gene pool, as most English Smooths are closely related.

I hope that in the search for the perfect blue merle we do not end up with a succession of badly marked merles, with heavy patches of white on the body. I would like to add that the eye problems associated with the defective whites has nothing to do with the hereditary eye problems which the Collie, of any colour, has as a breed. I personally think the white Collie, Rough or Smooth, is beautiful, providing the dog is of good quality. When I was in Switzerland I was invited to see a litter from Evelyne Mougeot's white Collie that she imported from America. I found them to be very attractive, and they all had dark eyes with good expression.

Chapter Eight

THE BREED STANDARD

For many years the Breed Standard of the Rough and of the Smooth Collie was identical, with the exception of the coat, and this remains the case with the American Breed Standard. However, in the UK, and in Australia, there are now separate Standards for the Rough and the Smooth Collie. I personally think this is a great shame. I believe the Rough Collie should still be bred for its working ability, as well as for its outstanding beauty, and I prefer the Breed Standard, agreed by the Conference of Collie Clubs in 1910.

THE CORRECT TYPE: STANDARD OF POINTS
Revised by the Collie Club, October 1898 and at the Conference of Collie Clubs, Crystal Palace, October 18th, 1910.

THE SKULL should be flat, moderately wide between the ears, and gradually tapering towards the eyes. There should only be a slight depression at the stop. The width of skull necessarily depends upon the combined length of skull and muzzle, and the whole must be considered in connection with the size of the dog. The cheek should not be full or prominent.

THE MUZZLE should be of fair length, tapering to the nose, and must not show weakness or be snipy or lippy. Whatever the colour of the dog may be, the nose must be black.

THE TEETH should be of good size, sound and level; very slight unevenness is permissible.

THE JAWS should be clean cut and powerful.

THE EYES are a very important feature, and give expression to the dog; they should be of medium size, set somewhat obliquely, of almond shape, and of a brown colour except in the case of Merle, when the eyes are frequently (one or both) blue and white or china; expression full of intelligence, with a quick alert look when listening.

THE EARS should be small and moderately wide at the base, and placed not too close together on top of the skull, nor too much to the side of the head. When in repose they should be usually carried thrown back, but when on the alert brought forward and carried semi-erect, with tip slightly drooping in attitude of listening. *FAULTS:* Length of head apparently out of proportion to the body and of the Borzoi type are to be strongly condemned. Weak, snipy muzzle, overshot mouth, heavy or gooseberry coloured, also glassy or staring eyes, are very objectionable. Domed skull, high-peaked occiput, prominent cheek, dish-faced, or Roman-nosed.

THE NECK should be muscular, powerful, and of fair length, and somewhat arched.

THE BODY should be rather long, with well sprung ribs, chest deep, fairly broad behind the shoulders, which should be sloped, loins slightly arched and powerful. The legs should be straight in front. *FAULTS:* Flat-sided, short, or cobby.

THE FORE LEGS should be straight and muscular, neither in nor out at elbows, with a fair amount of bone; the forearm somewhat fleshy, the pasterns showing flexibility without weakness. *FAULTS:* Weak, long pasterns, out at elbows, crooked forearms.

THE HIND LEGS should be muscular at the thighs, clean and sinewy below the hocks, with well bent stifles. *FAULTS:* Cowhocks, straight hocks.

THE FEET should be oval in shape, soles well padded and the toes arched and close together. The hind feet less arched, the hocks well let down and powerful. *FAULTS:* Large, open, flat, or hare feet, feet turned outwards or inwards.

THE BRUSH should be moderately long, carried low when the dog is quiet, with a slight upward 'swirl' at the end, and may be gaily carried when the dog is excited, but not over the back. *FAULTS:* Short tail, or tail carried over the back or twisted to one side.

THE COAT should be very dense, the outer coat harsh to the touch, the inner or under coat soft, furry, and very close, so close as to almost hide the skin. The mane and frill should be very abundant, the mask or face smooth, as also the ears at the tips, but they should carry more hair towards the base; the fore legs well feathered, the hind legs above the hocks profusely so; but below the hocks fairly smooth, although all heavily coated Collies are liable to grow a slight feathering. Hair on the brush very profuse. *FAULTS:* A soft, silky, or wavy coat, or insufficient undercoat.

COLOUR AND MARKING are immaterial, but other points being equal, a nice showily-marked dog is preferred. All white or Red Setter colour is most objectionable.

GENERAL CHARACTER: To enable the Collie to fulfil his natural bent for sheepdog work, he should be built on lines of strength, activity, and grace, with a shapely body and sound legs and feet. He should be lithe and active in his movements, and entirely free from cloddiness and coarseness in any part of his conformation; and lastly, he must be gifted with true expression. Expression is obtained by the perfect combination of head and muzzle, size, shape, and colour, and placement of eye, and correct position and carriage of ears, which gives the dog that sweet, dreamy, semi-cunning, yet alert outlook that makes the perfect Collie the most beautiful of the canine race.

SIZE AND WEIGHT: Dogs 22in to 24in at the shoulders, bitches 20in to 22in. Dogs 45 to 65lb, bitches 40 to 55lb.

The Smooth Collie only differs from the Rough in its coat, which should be hard, dense, and quite smooth.

THE COLLIE CLUB'S SCALE OF POINTS

Head and Expression	15
Ears	10
Neck and Shoulders	10
Legs and Feet	15
Hindquarters	10
Back and Loins	10
Brush	5
Coat and Frill	20
Size	5
TOTAL	100

Points of Anatomy

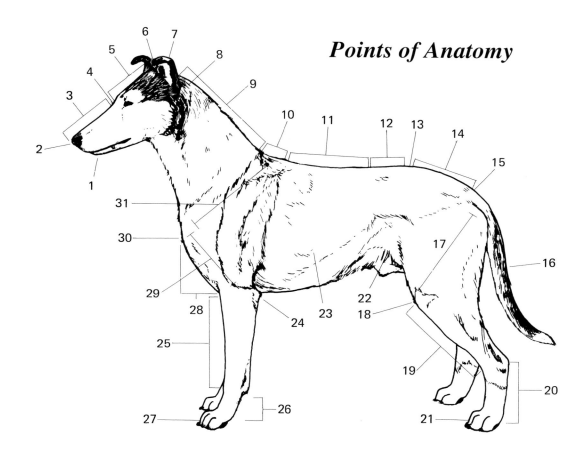

1. Underjaw
2. Nose
3. Muzzle
4. Stop
5. Skull
6. Occiput
7. Ear
8. Arch of Neck
9. Neck
10. Withers
11. Back
12. Loin
13. Hip bone
14. Croup
15. Set of Tail
16. Tail
17. Upper Thigh
18. Stifle joint
19. Second Thigh
20. Hock
21. Hind foot
22. Flank
23. Rib cage (Chest)
24. Elbow
25. Forearm
26. Pastern
27. Front foot
28. Brisket (Forechest)
29. Upper arm
30. Point of Shoulder
31. Shoulder

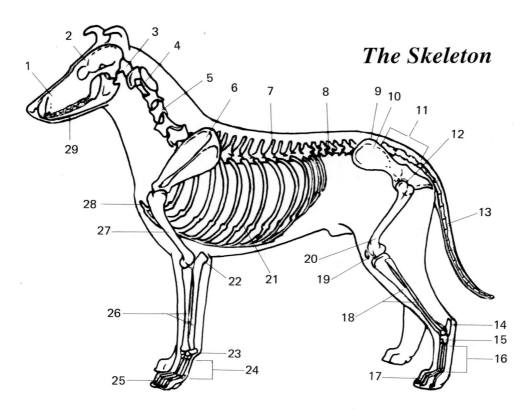

The Skeleton

1. Maxilla (upper jaw)
2. Cranium
3. Atlas vertebrae
4. Axis vertebrae
5. Cervical vertebrae
6. Scapula
7. Thoracic vertebrae
8. Lumbar vertebrae
9. Pelvis
10. Ilium
11. Croup
12. Hip joint
13. Coccygeal vertebrae
14. Hock joint
15. Tarsal bones
16. Metatarsal bones
17. Phalanges
18. Fibula Tibia
19. Patella
20. Femur
21. Ribs (13)
22. Olecranon
23. Carpal bones
24. Metacarpals
25. Phalanges
26. Radius Ulna (forearm)
27. Humerus (upper arm)
28. Sternum
29. Mandible (under jaw)

In the UK the Rough Collie and the Smooth Collie Breed Standards now have radical differences.

THE BRITISH BREED STANDARD: ROUGH COLLIE

GENERAL APPEARANCE Appears as dog of great beauty, standing with impassive dignity, with no part out of proportion to whole.

CHARACTERISTICS Physical structure on lines of strength and activity, free from cloddiness and with no trace of coarseness. Expression most important. In considering relative values it is obtained by perfect balance and combination of skull and foreface, size, shape, colour and placement of eyes, correct position and carriage of ears.

TEMPERAMENT Friendly disposition with no trace of nervousness or aggressiveness.

HEAD AND SKULL Head properties of great importance, must be considered in proportion to size of dog. Viewed from front or side, head resembles a well blunted clean wedge, being smooth in outline. Skull flat. Sides taper gradually and smoothly from ears to end of black nose, without prominent cheek bones or pinched muzzle. Viewed in profile, top of skull and top of muzzle lie in two parallel straight lines of equal length divided by a slight, but perceptible stop or break. A mid-point between inside corner of eyes (which is centre of a correctly placed stop) is centre of balance in length of head. End of smooth, well-rounded muzzle blunt, never square. Under jaw strong, clean-cut. Depth of skull from brow to underpart of jaw never excessive (deep through). Nose always black.

EYES Very important feature giving sweet expression. Medium size (never very small) set somewhat obliquely, of almond shape and dark brown colour, except in the case of blue merles when eyes are frequently (one or both, or part of one or both) blue or blue-flecked. Expression full of intelligence, with quick, alert look when listening.

EARS Small, not too close together on top of skull, nor too far apart. In repose carried thrown back, but on alert brought forward and carried semi-erect; that is with approximately two-thirds of ear standing erect, top third tipping forward naturally below horizontal.

MOUTH Teeth of good size. Jaws strong with a perfect, regular and complete scissor bite, i.e. upper teeth closely overlapping lower teeth and set square to jaws.

NECK Muscular, powerful, of fair length, well arched.

FOREQUARTERS Shoulders sloping and well angulated. Forelegs straight and muscular, neither in nor out at elbows, with moderate amount of round bone.

BODY Slightly long compared with height, back firm with slight rise over loins; ribs well sprung, chest deep, fairly broad behind shoulders.

HINDQUARTERS Hindlegs muscular at thighs, clean and sinewy below, with well bent stifles. Hocks well let down and powerful.

FEET Oval; soles well padded. Toes arched and close together. Hindfeet slightly less arched.

TAIL Long with bone reaching at least to hock joint. Carried low when quiet but with slight upward swirl at tip. May be carried gaily when excited, but never over back.

GAIT/MOVEMENT Distinctly characteristic in this breed. A sound dog is never out at the elbow, yet moves with front feet comparatively close together. Plaiting, crossing or rolling are highly undesirable. Hindlegs from hock joint to ground when viewed from rear to be parallel but not too close; when viewed from side, action is smooth. Hindlegs powerful with plenty of drive. A reasonably long stride is desirable and should be light and appear effortless.

COAT Fits outline of body, very dense. Outer coat straight and harsh to touch, undercoat soft, furry and very close, almost hiding the skin; mane and frill very abundant, mask and face smooth, ears smooth at tips, but carrying more hair towards base, front legs well feathered, but smooth below hock joint. Hair on tail very profuse.

COLOUR Three recognised colours: Sable and White, Tricolour and Blue Merle.

Sable: any shade of light gold to rich mahogany or shaded sable. Light straw or cream coloured highly undesirable.

Tricolour: predominantly black with rich tan markings about legs and head. A rusty tinge in topcoat highly undesirable.

Blue Merle: predominantly clear, silvery blue, splashed and marbled with black. Rich tan markings preferred but absence should not be penalised. Large black markings, slate colour, or rusty tinge either of top or undercoat are highly undesirable.

White markings: all above should carry typical white Collie markings to a greater or lesser degree. Following markings are favourable – white collar, full or part, white shirt, legs and feet, white tail tip. A blaze may be carried on muzzle or skull, or both.

SIZE Height: dogs 56-61 cm (22-24in) at shoulder; bitches 51-56 cm (20-22in).

FAULTS Any departure from the foregoing points should be considered a fault and the seriousness with which the fault should be regarded should be in exact proportion to its degree.

NOTE Male animals should have two apparently normal testicles fully descended into the scrotum.

Reproduced by kind permission of the English Kennel Club.

THE BRITISH BREED STANDARD: SMOOTH COLLIE

GENERAL APPEARANCE Appears as gifted with intelligence, alertness and activity. Stands with dignity governed by perfect anatomical formation, with no part out of proportion to whole, giving appearance of working capability.

CHARACTERISTICS Physical structure on lines of strength and activity, free from cloddiness and with no trace of coarseness. Expression most important. In considering relative values, it is obtained by perfect balance and combination of skull and foreface, size, shape, colour and placement of eyes, correct position and carriage of ears.

TEMPERAMENT Gay and friendly, never nervous nor aggressive.

HEAD AND SKULL Head properties of great importance, must be considered in proportion to size of dog. Viewed from front or side, head resembles a well blunted clean wedge, being smooth in outline. Skull flat. Sides taper gradually and smoothly from ears to end of black nose, without prominent cheek bones or pinched muzzle. Viewed in profile, top of skull and top of muzzle lie in two parallel straight lines of equal length divided by a slight, but perceptible stop or break. A mid-point between inside corner of eyes (which is centre of a correctly placed stop) is centre of balance in length of head. End of smooth, well-rounded muzzle blunt, never square. Under jaw strong, clean-cut. Depth of skull from brow to underpart of jaw never excessive (deep through). Nose always black.

EYES Very important feature giving sweet expression. Medium size (never very small) set somewhat obliquely, of almond shape and dark brown colour, except in the case of blue merles when eyes are frequently (one or both, or part of one or both) blue or blue-flecked. Expression full of intelligence, with quick, alert look when listening.

EARS Moderately large, wider at base, and placed not too close together nor too much on side of head. When in repose carried thrown back, but on alert brought forward and carried semi-erect, that is, with approximately two thirds of ear standing erect, top third tipping forward naturally, below horizontal.

MOUTH Teeth of good size. Jaws strong with a perfect, regular and complete scissor bite, i.e. upper teeth closely overlapping lower teeth and set square to jaws.

FOREQUARTERS Shoulders sloping and well angulated. Forelegs straight and muscular, neither in nor out at elbows, with moderate amount of bone. Forearm somewhat fleshy, pasterns showing flexibility without weakness.

BODY Slightly long compared with height, back firm with slight rise over loins; ribs well sprung, chest deep, fairly broad behind shoulders.

HINDQUARTERS Hindlegs muscular at thighs, clean and sinewy below, with well bent stifles. Hocks well let down and powerful.

FEET Oval; soles well padded. Toes arched and close together. Hindfeet slightly less arched.

TAIL Long with bone reaching at least to hock joint. Carried low when quiet but with slight upward swirl at tip. May be carried gaily when excited, but never over back.

GAIT/MOVEMENT Distinctly characteristic in this breed. A sound dog is never out at the elbow, yet moves with front feet comparatively close together. Plaiting, crossing or rolling are highly undesirable. Hindlegs from hock joint to ground when viewed from rear to be parallel but not too close; when viewed from side, action is smooth. Hindlegs powerful with plenty of drive. A reasonably long stride is desirable and should be light and appear effortless.

COAT Short, flat topcoat of harsh texture, with very dense undercoat. Not trimmed or clipped.

COLOUR Three recognised colours: Sable and White, Tricolour and Blue Merle.

Sable: any shade of light gold to rich mahogany or shaded sable. Light straw or cream coloured highly undesirable.

Tricolour: predominantly black with rich tan markings about legs and head. A rusty tinge in topcoat highly undesirable.

Blue Merle: predominantly clear, silvery blue, splashed and marbled with black. Rich tan markings preferred but absence should not be penalised. Large black markings, slate colour, or rusty tinge either of top or undercoat are highly undesirable.

White markings: all above should carry typical white Collie markings to a greater or lesser degree. Following markings are favourable – white collar, full or part, white shirt, legs and feet, white tail tip. A blaze may be carried on muzzle or skull, or both.

All white or predominantly white is most undesirable.

SIZE Height: dogs 56-61 cms (22-24ins) at shoulder; bitches 51-56 cms (20-22ins).

FAULTS Any departure from the foregoing points should be considered a fault and the seriousness with which the fault should be regarded should be in exact proportion to its degree.

NOTE Male animals should have two apparently normal testicles fully descended into the scrotum.

Reproduced by kind permission of the English Kennel Club.

Highlighting the major difference between the two Breed Standards, the 'General Appearance' section for for the Rough Collie states: "Appears as dog of great beauty, standing with impassive dignity, with no part out of proportion to whole." The equivalent section for the Smooth Collie

Ch. Rifflesea Reminds Me of Blu at Leckhill: the Rough Collie has a wealth of coat, but it should follow the same basic lines of conformation as the Smooth Collie.

Ch. Astrellita the Silversmith: Best of Breed at Crufts, 1983 and Top Smooth Collie of the Year, 1988. A beautifully constructed Smooth Collie.

Dalton.

states: "Appears gifted with intelligence, alertness and activity. Stands with dignity governed by perfect anatomical formation, with no part out of proportion, giving appearance of working ability." How unfair to state categorically that the Rough Collie should not have the appearance of working capabilities, or be alert and active. And these contrasts are reiterated throughout the two Standards. For instance:

SMOOTH COLLIE: "pasterns showing flexibility without weakness."
ROUGH COLLIE: No specific reference to pasterns.

SMOOTH COLLIE: "back level."
ROUGH COLLIE: "back firm."

SMOOTH COLLIE: "Gay and friendly."
ROUGH COLLIE: "Friendly disposition"

SMOOTH COLLIE: "EARS Moderately large,wider at the base."
ROUGH COLLIE: "EARS Small, not too close together."
  Yet the stipulations for the Head And Skull are identical.

SMOOTH COLLIE: "All white or predominantly white is most undesirable."
ROUGH COLLIE: No reference to white or predominantly white dogs.

The American Breed Standard combines the Rough and the Smooth, and I think it is superior to the British equivalent not only in this respect, but also because it gives a more overall picture. The American Standard allows white to be included as a permitted colour, with sable, tricolour or blue merle markings, whereas a predominantly white Collie would be heavily penalised everywhere else in the world. The FCI takes the British Breed Standard, as Britain is the breed's country of origin. In Australia there are separate Standards for the Rough and Smooth, and these vary slightly from the English versions. They have a separate section for Faults, which is as follows:
"FAULTS Length of head apparently out of proportion to body; receding skull or unbalanced head to be strongly condemned. Weak, snipey muzzle; domed skull; high peaked occiput, prominent cheek bones; dish-faced or Roman-nosed; under-shot or over-shot mouth; missing teeth; round or light coloured and glassy or staring eyes are highly objectionable. Body flat sided, short or cobby; straight shoulder or stifle; out at elbow; crooked fore-arms; cow-hocks or straight hocks, large, open or hare feet; feet turned in or out; long, weak pasterns; tail short, kinked or twisted to one side or carried over the back; a soft, silky or wavy coat or insufficient undercoat; prick ears, low-set ears; nervousness."

THE AMERICAN BREED STANDARD: ROUGH AND SMOOTH

GENERAL CHARACTER
The Collie is a lithe, strong, responsive active dog, carrying no useless timber, standing naturally straight and firm. The deep, moderately wide chest shows strength; the sloping shoulders and well bent hocks indicate speed and grace; the face shows high intelligence. The Collie presents an impressive, proud picture of true balance, each part being in harmonious proportion to every other part and to the whole. Except for the technical description that is

essential to this standard and without which no standard for the guidance of breeders and judges is adequate, it could be stated simply that no part of the Collie ever seems to be out of proportion to any other part. Timidity, frailness, sullenness, viciousness, lack of animation, cumbersome appearance and lack of overall balance impair the general character.

HEAD
The head properties are of great importance. When considered in proportion to the size of the dog, the head is inclined to lightness and never appears massive. A heavy headed dog lacks the bright, alert, full of sense look that contributes greatly to expression.

Both in front and in profile view the head bears a general resemblance to a well blunted clean wedge, being smooth and clean in outline and nicely balanced in proportion. On the sides, it tapers gradually and smoothly from the ears to the end of the black nose, without being flared out in the backskull (cheeky) or pinched muzzle (snipey). In profile view, the top of the backskull and the top of the muzzle lie in two approximately parallel, straight planes of equal length divided by a very slight but perceptible stop or break.

A mid point between the inside corners of the eyes (which is the center of a correctly placed stop) is the center of balance in length of head. The end of the smooth, well rounded muzzle is blunt but not square. The underjaw is strong, clean cut and the depth of skull from the brow to the underpart of the jaw is not excessive. The teeth are of good size meeting in a scissors bite. Overshot or undershot jaws are undesirable, the latter being more severely penalised. There is a very slight prominence of the eyebrows. The backskull is flat, without receding either laterally or backward and the occiputal bone is not highly peaked. The proper width of backskull necessarily depends upon the combined length of skull and muzzle, and the width of the backskull is less than its length. Thus the correct width varies with the individual and is dependent upon the extent to which it is supported by length of muzzle. Because of the importance of the head characteristics, prominent head faults are severely penalised.

EYES
Because of the combination of the flat skull, the arched eyebrows, the slight stop and the rounded muzzle, the foreface must be chiselled to form a receptacle for the eyes, and they are necessarily placed obliquely to give them the required forward outlook. Except for the blue merles they are required to be matched in colour. They are almond shaped, of medium size and never properly appear to be large or prominent. The colour is dark and the eye does not show a yellow ring or a sufficiently prominent haw to affect the dog's expression. The eyes have a clear, bright appearance, expressing intelligent inquisitiveness, particularly when the ears are drawn up and the dog is on the alert.

EARS
The ears are in proportion to the size of the dog's head and, if they are carried properly and unquestionably 'break' naturally, are seldom too small. Large ears usually cannot be lifted correctly off the head and even when lifted they will be out of proportion to the size of the head. When in repose, the ears are folded lengthwise and thrown back into the frill. On the alert, they are drawn well up on the backskull and are carried about three quarters erect with one fourth of the ear tipping or 'breaking' forward. A dog with prick ears or low ears cannot show true expression and is penalised accordingly.

NECK

The neck is firm, clean, muscular, sinewy and heavily frilled. It is fairly long, is carried upright with a slight arch at the nape and imparts a proud, upstanding appearance, showing off the frill.

BODY

The body is firm, hard and muscular, a trifle long in proportion to the height. The ribs are well rounded behind the well sloped shoulders and the chest is deep, extending to the elbows. The back is strong and level, supported by powerful hips and thighs and the croup is sloped to give a well rounded finish. The loin is powerful and slightly arched. Noticeably fat dogs, or dogs in poor flesh, or with disease, or with no undercoat are out of condition and moderately penalised acccordingly. In grown males, the monorchid and cryptorchid are disqualified.

LEGS

The forelegs are straight and muscular, with a fair amount of bone considering the size of the dog. A cumbersome appearance is undesirable. Both narrow and wide placement are penalised. The forearm is moderately fleshy and the pasterns are flexible, but without weakness. The hind legs are less fleshy, are muscular at the thighs, very sinewy, and the hocks and stifles well bent. A cow hocked dog or a dog with straight stifles is penalised. The comparatively small feet are approximately oval in shape. The soles are well padded and tough and the toes are well arched and close together.

When the Collie is not in motion, the legs and feet are judged by allowing the dog to come to a natural stop in a standing position so that both the forelegs and hind legs are placed well apart with the feet extending straight forward. Excessive 'posing' is undesirable.

GAIT

Gait is sound. When the dog is moved at a slow trot toward an observer, his straight front legs track comparatively close together at the ground. The front legs are not out at the elbow and do not 'cross' over, nor does the Collie move with a choppy, pacing, or rolling gait. When viewed from the rear, the hind legs are powerful and propelling. Viewed from the side, the reasonably long 'reaching' stride is smooth and even, keeping the back line firm and level. As the speed of the gait is increased, the Collie single tracks, bringing the front legs inward in a straight line from the shoulder toward the center line of the body. The gait suggests effortless speed combined with the dog's herding heritage, requiring it to be capable of changing its direction of travel almost instantaneously.

TAIL

The tail is moderately long, the bone reaching to the hock joint or below. It is carried low when the dog is quiet, the end having an upward twist or 'swirl'. When gaited or when the dog is excited it is carried gaily, but not over the back.

COAT

The well fitting, proper textured coat is the crowning glory of the Rough variety of Collie. It is abundant except on the head and legs. The outer coat is straight and harsh to the touch. A soft, open outer coat, or a curly outer coat is penalised, regardless of quantity. The undercoat, however, is soft, furry and so close together that it is difficult to see the skin when the hair is parted. The coat is very abundant on the mane and frill. The face or mask is smooth. The forelegs are smooth and well feathered to the back of the pasterns. The hind legs are smooth below the hock joints. Any feathering below the hocks is removed for the showring. The hair on the tail is very profuse and on the hips is long and bushy. The texture quantity and the extent to which the coat 'fits' the dog are important points.

COLOR

The four recognised colors are sable and white, tricolor, blue merle, and white. There is no preference among them. The sable and white is predominantly sable (a fawn, sable color of varying shades from light gold to dark mahogany) with white markings, usually on the chest, neck, legs, feet and tip of tail. A blaze may appear on the foreface or backskull, or both. The tricolor is predominantly black carrying white markings as in the sable and white, and has tan shadings on and about the head and legs. The blue merle is a mottled or 'marbled' color, predominantly blue grey and black, with white markings as in the sable and white, and usually has tan shadings as in the tricolor. The white is predominantly white with sable, tricolor or blue merle markings.

SIZE

Dogs are from 24 to 26 inches (61 to 66cm) at the shoulder and weigh from 60 to 75 pounds (27 to 33kg). Bitches are from 22 to 24 inches (55 to 60cm) at the shoulder, weighing from 50 to 65 pounds (22 to 27kg). An undersize or an oversize Collie is penalised according to the extent to which the dog appears to be undersize or oversize.

EXPRESSION

Expression is one of the most important points in considering the relative values of Collies. 'Expression' like the term 'character' is difficult to define in words. It is not a fixed point as in color, weight or height, and it is something the uninitiated can properly understand only by optical illustration. In general, however, it may be said to be the combined product of the shape and balance of skull and muzzle, the placement, size, shape and color of the eyes, and the position, size and carriage of the ears. An expression that shows sullenness or which is suggestive of any other breed is entirely foreign. The Collie cannot be judged properly until his expression has been carefully evaluated.

THE SMOOTH COLLIE

The Smooth Collie is judged by the same standard except for coat.
Reproduced by kind permission of the American Kennel Club.

INTERPRETATION AND ANALYSIS

GENERAL APPEARANCE

The British version gives no mention of the Rough Collie as a working dog, whereas the Smooth Collie is described as "giving appearance of working ability". This would, by implication, mean that the Rough Collie is obsolete as a working dog, and that it is incapable of carrying out a day's work. This, I believe, is a major omission. A true Collie should be able to run like the wind and change direction instantly; to turn on a sixpence. Most Rough Collies today are far too heavy to do this, and they also carry far too much soft coat, exaggerating the 'glamour' of the dog, and losing sight of its working ancestry. When I am judging, I like my male winners to be masculine in appearance with no coarseness, and I like my bitch winners to be feminine, but sound.

The physical structure of the Rough and the Smooth Collie, should be the same, according to the Breed Standard. In fact, the Smooth Collie carries all the characteristics of strength and activity and can still do the job it was bred for, whereas the Rough Collie is now bred purely as a show dog – a very beautiful show dog – but with far too much coat to be able to work a day with sheep, in the pouring rain. Over the years many breeders have concentrated on breeding the perfect head and eye, and as much coat as possible, forgeting that the Collie does not need these features in order to do a full day's work.

The Collie, Rough or Smooth, is a Sheepdog built on lines of strength and activity. The dignity should always be obvious, both in male and female. The Collie is a proud animal who shows great beauty where nothing is excessive or extreme.
A true Collie must be balanced all over.

This male corresponds to the Standard from tip of nose to tip of tail. He is soundly constructed and stands with dignity. He has a clean smooth wedge head, and the correct amount of coat fitting body shape.

A dog with correct bone and coat, but has straight shoulders, short neck, sloping topline, ribcage not deep enough, weak in loins, and lacking the harmony and balance between front and hindquarters.

Shows the dignity of the true Collie type, but is too heavily built and lacking angulation in front and behind. This dog tends to be coarse all over.

A common type of Collie today, slightly feminine, lacking dignity. Incorrect in overall construction with bad front, weak hindquarters and hindlegs tucked under body. The coat is soft and not straight enough, and a little short all over.

Head without dignity and feminine. Untypical abundant coat covering a badly constructed Collie who would be unfit to work.

A Collie that lacks the lines of strength, activity and elegance, with an extremely short neck and a bad front giving the impression that the head comes directly from the shoulders.

The long coat over the croup makes this Collie look reasonably long, but on closer inspection this is not the case. The dog lacks strength in the hindquarters. The front is straight and the neck lacks arch. The head is short with a fine muzzle.

CHARACTERISTICS AND TEMPERAMENT

The temperament of the Rough and the Smooth Collie is basically the same, in that they are both loving and loyal. The Smooth Collie is more agile, possibly more inquisitive, and sometimes noisier. However, it is always difficult to assess how strong an influence the home environment is on the indiviual Collie's temperament.

HEAD AND SKULL

In Britain, far too much emphasis is placed upon the head properties, so much so that many judges will sacrifice all else just for a pretty head and a sweet expression. I have lost count of the number of times that I have read critiques where the body shape and movement of the dog is hardly mentioned. For example: "beautiful headed dog, lovely expression, good stop, rounded muzzle, neat ears carried well, rather lethargic on the move, could not be denied his placing today." There is no mention whatsoever about body-lines, shoulders, feet, bend of stifle etc. Collies, both Rough and Smooth, are deemed to be 'head breeds', and while a good head and eye is very important, I see no point in breeding good heads on unsound bodies.

Ladyfare Blue Lagoon at Kavara: Note the neat ear carriage and beautiful expressive eyes.

Astrellita Alicia: Viewed from the front, the head should resemble a well blunted clean wedge. An imaginary line drawn from the outer corner of the eyes to the base of the ears gives the desired expression. Note the correct placement of the ears.

The correct Collie head.

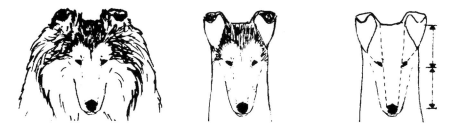

Correctly formed and balanced head, resembling from the front a clean, smooth wedge with rounded well-filled muzzle and flat skull, which is not too strong.

Correct length of head, but the skull is too strong and flares out. The foreface is correct with nicely rounded and well-filled muzzle.

Correct length of head and correct skull, but the foreface is too snipey, with a pinched muzzle, which makes the head look a little over-long, even if it is not.

The head is too short all over, and it has lost dignity and elegance.

Short head with a pinched muzzle set into a skull that tends to widen and ears set too far apart.

Head is too short and coarse, with strong skull and muzzle, lacks all the dignity and elegance of the breed.

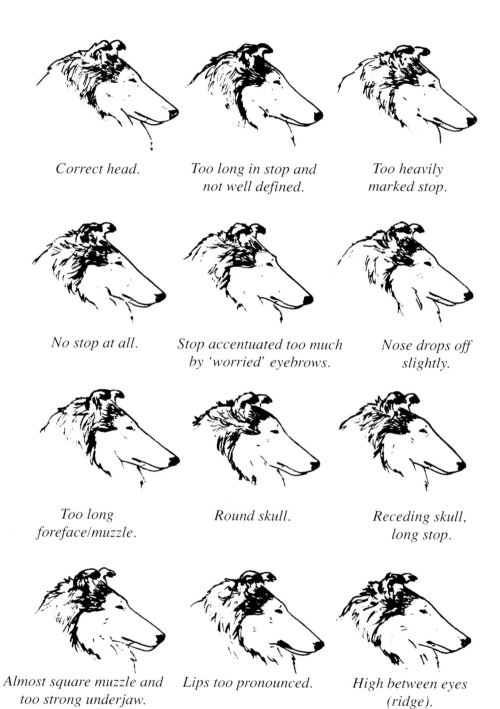

Correct head.

Too long in stop and
not well defined.

Too heavily
marked stop.

No stop at all.

Stop accentuated too much
by 'worried' eyebrows.

Nose drops off
slightly.

Too long
foreface/muzzle.

Round skull.

Receding skull,
long stop.

Almost square muzzle and
too strong underjaw.

Lips too pronounced.

High between eyes
(ridge).

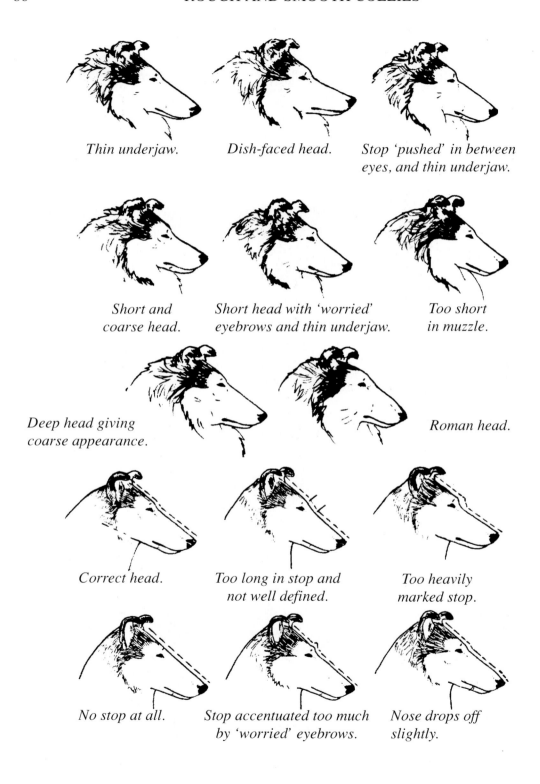

Thin underjaw.

Dish-faced head.

Stop 'pushed' in between eyes, and thin underjaw.

Short and coarse head.

Short head with 'worried' eyebrows and thin underjaw.

Too short in muzzle.

Deep head giving coarse appearance.

Roman head.

Correct head.

Too long in stop and not well defined.

Too heavily marked stop.

No stop at all.

Stop accentuated too much by 'worried' eyebrows.

Nose drops off slightly.

*Too long
foreface/muzzle.*

Round skull.

*Receding skull,
long stop.*

*Almost square muzzle
and too strong underjaw.*

Lips too pronounced.

*High between eyes
(ridge).*

Thin underjaw.

Dish-faced head.

*Stop 'pushed' in between
eyes, and thin underjaw.*

*Short and
coarse head.*

*Short head with 'worried'
eyebrows and thin underjaw.*

*Too short in
muzzle.*

Deep head giving coarse appearance.

Roman head.

Correct head in shape and balance but should not be any stronger. The ears are well-set, but too big and heavy. Alert expression.

Short head with blunt muzzle, but lips too pronounced in front. Wide skull. Expression a little hard, triangular eyes, wide (broad ears).

Short head with an expression that is foreign to the breed. Small eyes, skull too wide and 'spongy', stop too pronounced, dish-faced head and lips hanging out in front.

Head that is more like a triangle than a wedge, with a broad skull. Ears heavy, head a little deep. Friendly expression, underjaw could be stronger.

Correct head in shape, which shows the desired smoothness of lines, with a flat skull and rounded foreface. Well placed eyes of correct size and shape, good ears, typical expression.

Erratic expression with round eyes. Head tends to be a little strong and full between eyes. Ears correctly placed, but a little too heavy.

A 'sweet' expression, but not what the Standard asks for. Eyes set straight, 'worried' eyebrows, short head that lacks elegance, broad skull, wide and heavy ears.

Very big ears which are also too heavy. Shorter type of head that could be longer and fuller in muzzle. Thin underjaw and lips hanging in front.

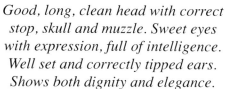

Good, long, clean head with correct stop, skull and muzzle. Sweet eyes with expression, full of intelligence. Well set and correctly tipped ears. Shows both dignity and elegance.

The receding skull and the long stop are the main faults, and so the head can never have the true wedge shape when viewed from the side.

Flat skull and good ears, but the stop and muzzle are very long, with nose 'pointing' out. Round eyes, and underjaw could be stronger.

Shows no resemblance to a wedge. 'Spongy' skull which is slightly round, and 'worried' eyebrows. Stop too pronounced and nose drops off slightly. Well marked underjaw but lips are not clean cut. A coarse head without finesse.

Skull too strong, stop too pronounced, which makes the head look divided. Ears too big, but well-set. Quite a good eye, but the head has an overall coarse impression.

Good length head showing wedge shape, but it is too hard cut and strong in lines, with marked cheekbones, stop too long, lips too pronounced. Well-set ears, expression could be sweeter.

Strongly dish-faced head that has totally lost the desired shape and is far from what the Standard asks for. Too short in skull and underjaw could be stronger. Lacking in dignity.

This may appear like a sweet head, but it has many faults. It is too short all over, it is triangular from the side, the stop is too marked, the underjaw could be stronger. The ears are too big, wide-set and heavy.

EYES

The eyes should be almond-shaped and set obliquely. This not only looks correct, it also enables the dog to have full vision. It is difficult to describe the correct Collie expression and the importance of the eyes in creating this, but in order to achieve that soft, dreamy look, the outer corner of the eye should slope upwards to meet the outer corner of the ear base, and the inner corner of the eye should slope upwards to meet the inner corner base of the ear. However, most of all, the eyes should look bright, intelligent and alert.

The correct eye of the Rough Collie should be dark brown in colour, medium-sized, set a little obliquely, giving a sweet expression which is also full of intelligence. The dog should look alert when it is at attention and listening. Different eyes can change the expression on the same head.

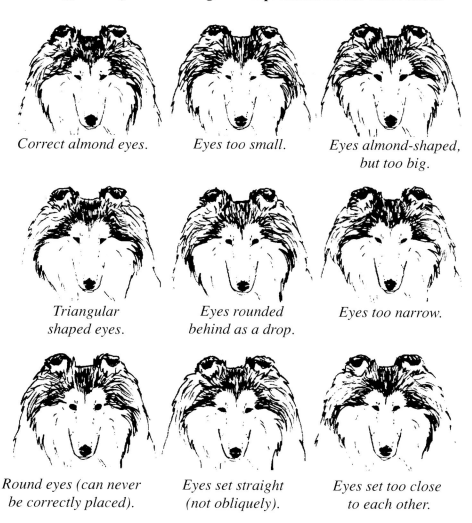

Correct almond eyes.

Eyes too small.

Eyes almond-shaped, but too big.

Triangular shaped eyes.

Eyes rounded behind as a drop.

Eyes too narrow.

Round eyes (can never be correctly placed).

Eyes set straight (not obliquely).

Eyes set too close to each other.

EARS

To assess the correct ear carriage and placement, the inside edge of the ear at base should be directly above the eye. Smooth Collie ears appear to be bigger but, in fact, this is only because of the lack of hair, and a Rough Collie's ears are somewhat low-set, whereas the Smooths carry their ears erect (always 'on the listen').

Correct ears contribute to the Collie's expression, and they also accentuate the wedge shape of the head.

Well-set, correctly shaped and correctly carried ears of the right size.

Ears of correct size, but set too close (the wedge shape is lost).

Ears of correct size and shape, but set too far apart (again, wedge shape is lost).

Prick ears.

Ears too heavy, although they are fairly well-set.

Ears too big, but well-carried and well-set.

Light ears, they should tip a little more.

MOUTH
One thing I hate to see on any Collie is a loose lip-line. I find it spoils the whole appearance of the face.

NECK
A well arched neck is equally important on the Rough and the Smooth Collie. However, if there is a fault in this area it is far more obvious on the Smooth Collie as they do not have a mane of hair.

FOREQUARTERS
Obviously any faults in conformation are immediately obvious in the Smooth Collie. Legs must be strong and straight in order for the Collie to stand and move correctly.

The ideal angle of the shoulder blade is around 45 to 50 degrees to the horizontal, which is also the ideal angle for the upper arm (humerus).

This dog shows total balance in the forequarters. In well-balanced forequarters a vertical line can be drawn from the top of the shoulder to the elbow.

This dog is too straight in the shoulder (around 55 degrees), and also too straight in the upper arm (around 60 degrees). Note that the height at the withers in this dog has become several centimetres higher because of the straight shoulder and upper arm.
The size and general construction of the dogs is the same.

The Collie, Rough and Smooth, seen from the front, should have straight front legs, neither in nor out at the elbows, and the ribcage should be formed with the correct amount of depth.

Correct

Incorrect

Slightly out at elbows, caused by too round a ribcage.

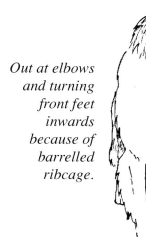

Out at elbows and turning front feet inwards because of barrelled ribcage.

Front legs very narrow and standing too close together. The ribcage is too narrow which makes the front feet turn outwards.

BODY

The body of the Smooth Collie must be balanced, with no outstanding faults, as, again, it does not have the long coat of the Rough Collie to cover any defects. However, the Rough Collie should not have a 'huge' coat. Although the coat is long, it should still be possible to see a perfect outline without having to search for it under a mountain of hair. Good shoulders are a must for both the Rough and the Smooth Collie, as are well-sprung ribs, and a deep chest. I like to see a good length of back. Handlers should never string up a Collie like a Terrier; it makes the Collie looks as though it has long legs and a 'chicken' neck.

HINDQUARTERS

It is not often that you see a cow hocked Collie these days; I am happy to say this fault has become quite rare. Some years ago many Collies had very long hocks, and were often prone to having cow hocks. Now, many Collies have strong, short hocks, giving more strength.

FEET

To my mind, feet are just as important as head, eye, or expression. In order for a Collie to move with purpose, and to be agile in its working role, feet must play an important part. Strong, oval, well-padded feet are a must; nothing is worse than seeing thin hare-like feet on a Collie.

TAIL

A tail carried in a curl over the back is unforgivable; not only is it unsightly, but it also spoils the whole outline of the Collie on the move. When I am judging the Rough or the Smooth Collie, this is one fault I have to penalise severely. A tail that is carried high is acceptable; a tail that is carried gaily if the dog is happy is acceptable, but it must never be curled over the back.

GAIT/MOVEMENT

The movement of a Collie, Rough or Smooth, is characteristic of the breed. A sound dog is never out at the elbow, yet it moves with its front feet comparatively close together. Plaiting, crossing, or rolling are highly undesirable.

Seen from behind, the hindquarters should be parallel, with strong, short hocks.

Cow-hocked, with the hocks turning in and the feet turning out.

Very close hindquarters due to narrow hip bones with high hocks.

A trio of Steadlyn Rough Collies showing correct flowing movement.　　　　*Pro Dog.*

The carriage and correct set of tail depend on many factors, and the illustrations show how tail set and bone formation can affect the carriage of the tail.

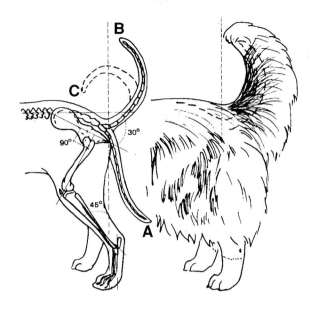

Totally correct hindquarters with the right length of croup (croup meaning the last three vertebrae, before those of the tail, which have grown together into one bone), and a well-set tail of good length with long vertebrae making the tail more rigid so it can only lift 30 degrees.
Tail A: The dog is standing relaxed.
Tail B: The maximum that this tail can move up to, which is correct, as the tail is not over the dotted line.
Tail C. This tail is too 'soft' as it can curl too much. It is well-set, but it is carried over the back because of its softness. A profusely coated tail can look more curled due to the fall of the coat.

A very sloping hip bone and a short croup, making the tail higher set in the hindquarters. This type of hindquarters leads to less muscular thighs and incorrect angulation, with less powerful and smooth movement. Tail C shows the softer type of tail.

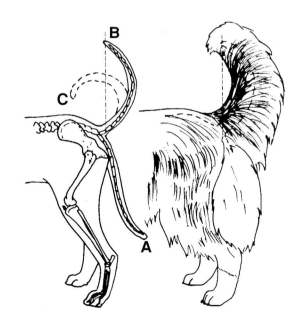

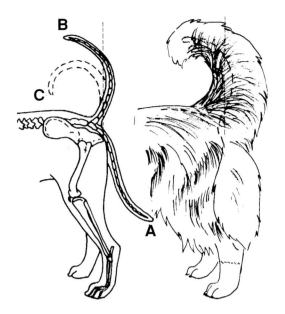

The hip bone is long enough, and the croup is of an adequate length, but the angle of both the hip bone and croup means that the tail (even when stiffer) will be too high-set and carried over the back. Tail C is even worse because of its softness. A straight hip bone also gives less angulation to the hindquarters.

The Breed Standard states the the tail should be 'carried low when quiet, with a slight upward swirl at the tip, may be carried gaily when excited, but never over back.' The Standard states 'not over back', but it does not state 'over the line of the back' so how should the Standard be interpreted? With the type and set of tail that a Collie has, it would be impossible for the tail to be carried over the line of the back (horizontal line).

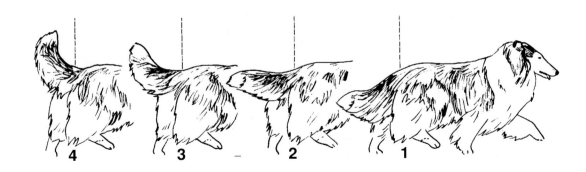

Dogs 1, 2, 3 and 4 all tails which are correctly carried, correctly set, and of good length.

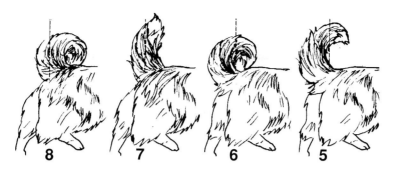

Dog 5 has a well-set tail, but it is carried too high over the back. Dog 6 has a well-set tail, but it is curled over the back. Dog 7 has a tail that is too high-set, although it is carried straight. Dog 8 has a high-set tail that is also curly.

When viewed from the rear, the hind legs from the hock joint to the ground should be parallel but not too close. When viewed from the side, the action must be smooth. The hind legs should be powerful, with plenty of drive. A reasonably long stride is desirable; it should be light and appear quite effortless. A well-constructed Collie, Rough or Smooth, that moves with drive, on sound, well-padded feet is absolute poetry in motion.

COAT
Most Smooth Collies have good coats, harsh to the touch, with a dense undercoat. This should not to be confused with an open coat, which is undesirable in a Smooth. Many Rough Collie coats today are far too soft and fluffy, due to the fact that many breeders try to breed for a fuller coat. However, nothing is so ungainly as seeing a Collie that is burdened with a mass of coat; it completely spoils the outline of the dog – and when you are judging, you have to 'dig deep' to find the dog. These 'fluffy' dogs take ages to dry if they get wet, whereas a Collie with the correct coat will just shake off the excess water.

COLOUR
The black on a tricolour must be jet black, with no hint of rustiness to spoil the density of the colour. Blue merles should be a silvery blue; slate or dark grey merles are not desirable. A white blaze on the face is perfectly acceptable, but while this marking is quite common on the Smooth Collie, it is rarely seen on the Rough Collie.

SIZE
When measuring the height of a Collie, Rough or Smooth, it should be taken from the withers to the ground.

SUMMARY
When I judge the Rough Collie I am looking for a proud upstanding Collie, with a correct length of head, a sweet, intelligent expression, a well-arched neck set into well-laid shoulders; good length of body, sound, but elegant; strong, well-boned legs; strong, well-padded feet; a good bend of stifle and well let-down hocks, and covered in a harsh, well-fitting jacket, giving an overall picture of dignity. To me, that is the Rough Collie.

Chapter Nine

GROOMING

Grooming is one of the most rewarding pastimes, and preparing your Collie for the show ring is part of the excitement of show-going. However, it is equally important for pet-owners to keep their dogs in good condition, and obviously a Rough Collie, with its beautiful long coat, will need regular grooming sessions.

GROOMING THE PET COLLIE

The primary purpose of grooming is to stimulate a dog's skin and to rid the coat of dead hair. A Smooth Collie will therefore benefit from being groomed, but it is essentially a low-maintenance breed that will require the minimum attention. This is not the case with a Rough Collie. If a Rough Collie is not groomed regularly its coat will knot and tangle. This not only looks awful, it causes discomfort to the dog.

   The tools that are needed are: .
1. A good-quality brush. It is worth investing in a bristle brush, although they are expensive; nylon or wire brushes tend to tear the coat and leave dead dry ends.
2. A fine-toothed comb.
3. A wide-toothed comb.
4. Scissors.
5. Nail cutters.

BATHING

Do not bath your Collie too often as this will remove all the natural oils in the coat. In fact, if you brush your Collie regularly, one bath a year at moulting time will be sufficient. If you do need to bath your Collie, prepare everything in advance, as once in the bath your Collie should never be left alone. Make sure you have plenty of warm water, shampoo, and lots of towels ready before you start. There are many different brands of dog shampoo on the market, including the insecticidal types, and you can choose whichever shampoo is appropriate.

   If you are using your own bath, place a rubber mat on the base of the bath. This not only stops the Collie slipping, but it also safeguards the bottom on your bath from scratch marks. Start off with a few inches of water in the bath, and then put the Collie into the water and pour water over the dog's coat, using a jug, until the dog is thoroughly wet. I always mix the shampoo into some water for easy lathering, and then I gently lather the dog all over, making sure no water goes into his eyes or ears. You can put some cotton wool in the ears, but do make sure to take it out again as soon as the bath is over.

Massage the coat gently, taking care to wash under the belly and tail area, and right down to the tip of the tail. If you are using an insecticidal shampoo, leave it on for a few minutes to soak into the skin. Then thoroughly rinse the shampoo off, over and over again, until every last bit of lather has gone. Before taking the dog from the bath, slip a dry towel over the coat and take off some of the excess water, as when a Collie starts to shake, water goes everywhere! When you have got rid of the excess water you can dry your Collie using a hair dryer. As you dry, start brushing from under the belly, finishing with the head and the ears.

When your Collie is almost dry, you can get to work on grooming the beautiful clean coat. Start from the back, working your way forwards, brushing upwards against the lay of the coat. In this way, any mats or tangles will soon loosen. Make sure you brush under the belly and armpits as this is where tangles can occur, and then brush the feathers on the legs. You may need to trim the hair between the pads, and for this job you will need to take a pair of blunt-ended scissors. Cut off any excess hair between the pads, taking great care not to cut the dog.

You can use this opportunity to check if the nails need cutting. If they are too long, use your nail cutters and just trim the tips of the nails. Make sure you do not cut into the quick, as this will make the nail bleed. If this does happen, put a little permanganate of potash to the end of a dampened cotton bud and apply to the affected nail – this will soon stem the bleeding. To complete the grooming, check your dog's teeth to see if they need cleaning. You can buy specially manufactured dog toothpaste, although human toothpaste is equally good. I have always found that a little peroxide, mixed with water and then brushed over the teeth, works wonders.

PREPARING THE ROUGH COLLIE FOR SHOW
The art of preparation takes a while to learn but is well worth the effort, as a well-groomed Collie is most important if you wish to win with your Collie. Clever grooming can also hide the odd fault. One week before the show, trim your Collie's nails and remove any excess hair from the pads, making a neat-shaped foot. Trim the hocks lightly so as to give a clean shape. This is done by brushing out the hair away from the hock, and taking a pair of blunt-ended scissors to trim the excess hair. Make sure you do not cut the hair too short, as this gives an impression of the dog having thin legs. Remember to trim a little at a time until you are satisfied with the result. During the week leading up to the big day, clean the ears and, using finger and thumb, remove dead hair from behind the ears, making sure there are no knots. Never trim the ears, as this will give a hard look and spoil your Collie's expression.

You want to present a clean, sweet-smelling dog in the ring, but it is not a good idea to bath your Collie too frequently. Whether it is a pet dog or a show dog, an annual bath at moulting time is sufficient. However, the day before the show I always wash all white parts of the Collie's coat – the mane and the legs – using a good dog shampoo. Human shampoo is not suitable as it could well irritate your Collie's skin. While the coat is still damp I apply a light dusting of magnesium carbonate BP, which is a very fine powder. This helps to give a stand-off coat, which is so attractive on the Collie. Remember that before you go to the show, every trace of powder must be removed with a brush.

Make sure that your Collie's teeth are clean and that its breath is sweet-smelling. There is nothing worse than seeing teeth caked with food, and this is usually the cause of bad breath. If you have prepared your Collie at home, all you have to do before you go into the ring is to give the dog a quick brush over and you are ready. I always use a coat dressing just before going into the ring, as this gives the final finish to an otherwise clean dog. There are many coat dressings on the market, but I believe there is nothing like soft rainwater and a little bay rum for making a Collie's

Ch. Jeffield Esquire: beautifully groomed ready for the show ring.

coat shine. In my early days of showing, I saw Derek Smith of the Clickham Collies grooming a dog for the ring, and it was a lesson just to watch him at work. The Collie took shape before your eyes – it was sheer magic. Derek first dampened the Collie's coat with a very fine spray, and then he packed a fine white powder into the white parts of the neck and legs and feet, paying special attention to the feathering. He then started to brush the Collie from the back end to the front, finishing with the neck and mane; the feathering on the Collie's legs stood out like silk and the coat, that was quite ordinary to begin with, was transformed to an abundance framing the Collie's lovely head. The bitch was Saheltras Sally Sunshine of Clickham, who went on to become an English Champion before going to the kennels of Luciano Bernini in Italy.

PREPARING THE SMOOTH COLLIE FOR SHOW

Just because the Smooth Collie has a short coat, it does not mean you can skimp on preparation before a show – there is still plenty to do, although it is not so time-consuming. A Smooth Collie should always be shown in pristine condition, with its coat gleaming.

Make sure the coat is clean and all the white parts are spotless. The night before a show you should wash all the white parts of your Collie. Rub your dog down well and groom thoroughly. I always use a pure silk scarf on my Smooths as it brings the coat up beautifully. One thing I cannot abide is a Smooth Collie with long dirty toe nails, so I always pay special attention to the feet –

Ch. Newarp Dark Crusader: a typical tricolour male with excellent markings. Note how the handler, Sara Pettit, (Junior Handler of the Year), enhances the overall picture by wearing clothes to complement the dog.

Lyn Howell.

remember they have no feathers to hide them. The teeth should also be checked to make sure they are clean.

The Smooth Collie has to go all-out to beat the Rough Collie, so make sure your Smooth Collie is gleaming. You must remember that on a Smooth, everything shows; there is no long fur to cover any faults. It is also important to remember that it is an insult to show your dog in a dirty condition under any judge.

THE HANDLER

Now you must prepare yourself for the show ring, and the same grooming programme applies. Plan what to wear to complement your Collie, and choose something that will give you confidence, because if you are confident it will give your dog confidence. Never wear high heels in the ring, and never wear lots of jangling bracelets or strong-smelling perfume – all dogs dislike perfume. Flowing skirts also cause problems because they obscure the dog's outline and the skirt can blow into the dog's face causing it to move badly.

If you take all these things into consideration, you should not go far wrong. If you do not have a big win, then at least you will know that you have done your very best and you have handled a well-trained, well-groomed Collie. Remember that you take home the same dog as you started out with, regardless of whether you win a major prize or not. It is more important that you are satisfied with your dog's performance.

Chapter Ten

THE SHOW RING

Exhibiting dogs is a fascinating and satisfying pastime; you will make many friends, experience triumphs and disappointments, as well as having all the fun of owning and breeding beautiful dogs. If you wish to own a successful kennel of Rough or Smooth Collies then showing is essential. You cannot offer dogs at stud, or puppies for sale, if you are unknown and have no reputation within the breed. A reputation is something that can only be built up slowly, over a period of years. You may be very lucky and have beginner's luck, but unless it is widely known that your dogs produce winning stock, or that you are known to sell show-winning stock, success will be well nigh impossible. I personally know of no better way of spending a weekend than to be at a dog show, in the company of my many doggy friends. This is a hobby which takes you right out of your normal routine, and you can forget about all the pressures of work or domestic responsibilities. After over a quarter of a century spent going to shows, I wonder if there are any excuses left to use when a midweek Championship show occurs (in theory, I have no relations left – and I come from a very big family!). You soon learn to shop when you can, fill the freezer full of pre-cooked meals, and in the summer, when the show season is in full swing, I leave my photograph on the mantelpiece and my voice on the answering machine!

Regular exhibitors have many stories to tell of their experiences at dog shows – I am sure I am not the only person who has taken the wrong dog to a show, and I have also gone to the wrong venue! One of my most memorable experiences was getting caught in a snow storm en route to the LKA Championship Show in 1990. I was with fellow exhibitor Lyn Westby in a car full of Rough Collies, Smooth Collies and Chihuahuas, when we got stuck in a snow drift. We were rescued four hours later by a farmer in a Land Rover. He took us to the nearest Police Station, where we spent the night with our dogs, underneath the canteen billiard table – we never got to the show!

Like every exhibitor, you must accept from the beginning of your showing career that your dog is not going to win every time it is entered at a show. One year, for instance, my Collie won Best Bitch at Crufts – one of the highest honours you can achieve in the show world – only to be thrown out of a Championship show a few weeks later without even being placed!

BRITAIN

TYPES OF SHOWS
MATCHES: These are held under Kennel Club rules, and dogs are selected on a knock-out basis – winner continues to meet winner until one dog is the final winner. Most of these matches are organised by local ringcraft societies.

EXEMPTION SHOWS: This type of show is exempt from KC rules, but a KC licence is still needed to hold the show. They are restricted to four pedigree classes, and the remainder is made up of variety classes. The shows are usually run in aid of a charity; they are great fun, and provide a good opportunity for the beginner to learn more about the show scene. They are also useful as a training ground for young dogs – dogs which have already won a CC in the show ring are prohibited from entering.

SANCTION SHOWS: Entry is restricted to twenty classes and is confined to members of the society or club organising the show. No Champions are allowed to enter.

LIMITED SHOWS: This type of show is also confined to club members, but there are usually more classes on offer. There are often a number of fun variety classes on offer.

OPEN SHOWS: This type of show is open to all pedigree dogs that are registered with the Kennel Club. This is usually much larger than the Limited Show, and sometimes an All Breed Society will stage as many as 250 classes. The more popular breeds are regularly given their own classes, but very few societies put on classes for Smooth Collies. If there are several Smooth Collie breeders in the area then the local society will classify the breed, but usually Smooths have to enter 'Any Variety Not Separately Classified' or 'Any Variety Working', which gives you the chance of exhibiting under two separate judges.

CHAMPIONSHIP SHOWS: These are highly competitive, as so much more is at stake, for this is where Challenge Certificates (CCs) are awarded and Champions are made up. This is also where qualifying classes are held for the forthcoming Crufts Dog Show – the UK's premier canine event. Anyone may enter a Championship Show with a KC registered dog, and the shows can be staged by specialist breed clubs or they can be general all breed shows.

Classes at a Championship are usually as follows:

PUPPY: 6 to 9 months.

PUPPY: 9 to 12 months.

JUNIOR: 6 to 18 months.

NOVICE: Any dog who has not won a CC or three or more first prizes at Championship shows.

POST GRADUATE: For all Collies who have not won a CC or five or more first prizes at Championship shows.

LIMIT: For all Collies who have not won three CCs under three different judges, or seven or more prizes in all.

OPEN: All Collies can be entered in this class.

VETERAN: For all Collies of seven years of age or over.

Each class has a winner; all winners are called into the ring after the open class, and from these winners a best dog or bitch is chosen. At a Championship Show the best dog and bitch would be the CC winners. The best dog then competes against the best bitch for the Best of Breed, and the winner will go forward to be judged in the Group (i.e. the Working Group), and if selected will go forward to compete against the other Group winners for Best in Show.

TO BECOME CHAMPION

In order to become a Champion, a dog must be awarded three CCs under three different judges. A dog can only gain its title when it is twelve months of age. Unlike the continent, the CC winner can come from any class of the day, providing CCs are on offer for the breed.

AMERICA

In America the Rough and Smooth Collie are classified as one breed. They have the same Breed Standard, simply highlighting the different lengths of coat between the two varieties. In contrast with Europe and the UK, registration documents do not state whether the Collie is Rough or Smooth. Each sex is judged separately in the following classes:

PUPPIES: 6 to 9 months of age.
PUPPIES: 9 to 12 months of age.
NOVICE CLASS: For dogs who have never won a first prize in an adult class.
EXHIBITOR BRED: All Collies 6 months or over, except Champions, and must be exhibited by the owner or partnership, and bred by them.
USA BRED: All Collies bred in the USA, except Champions.
OPEN CLASS: All Collies over 6 months, including Champions and imports, but most American Champions are only shown in the special class.
SPECIAL CLASS: American Champions.

TO BECOME A CHAMPION

The winners of each class compete against each other for the title Winner and Reserve Winner. It is only the Winner who is awarded points. Champions are made up by a points system and the amount of points won depends on how many Collies of the same sex the winner has defeated in the class. Points also vary depending on geographical regions.

To become an American Champion a dog must win fifteen points under a minimum of three different judges, including two major shows under different judges. Five points is the maximum that can be won at any given show.

EUROPE

All over Europe dog shows and dog breeding are controlled by the Federation Cynologique International (FCI). Judging procedures are different in that each dog entered must be judged on its own and given a critique before leaving the ring. There are two types of FCI shows: the Certificat d'Aptitude Championat International Beaute (CACIB) certificates are awarded at the International shows, and national certificates are awarded at CAC shows.

On the continent there are usually four classes: PUPPY, JUNIOR and OPEN, followed by CHAMPION. Dogs are judged individually and graded as:
'Excellent' – for a Collie that fits the Breed Standard.
'Very Good' – for a Collie with minor faults but suitable for breeding.
'Good' – for a Collie that is sadly lacking quality and should not be bred from. In some countries three such prizes would mean breeding is prohibited.

Puppies are not allowed to win CCs or Reserve CCs, but may be awarded Best of Breed.

TO BECOME A CHAMPION

Rules for becoming a CAC National Champion differ in each country. In Scandinavian countries a Collie, Rough or Smooth, cannot become a full Champion until the dog has passed a temperament test, which is designed to prove the mental stability of dog. Two judges approach the dog to check that it is friendly, and then bags or sacks filled with empty tin cans are thrown to the ground to test the reaction of the Collie. Sometimes open umbrellas or even bells are thrown to the ground and the Collies have to walk among them. The next stage of the test is for two people, often dressed in a uniform or overalls, to approach the dog firing guns in the air, to check if the Collie is gun-shy. The Collie must not panic or show any aggression; if it attacks, it will fail the test.

TO BECOME AN INTERNATIONAL CHAMPION
To gain this title, a Collie, Rough or Smooth, must win four CACIBs in three different countries, and two of these must be won where the Collie resides. The CACIBS must be won under different judges.

AUSTRALIA AND NEW ZEALAND
To become an Australian Champion a Collie, Rough or Smooth, must amass 100 points at shows, plus four CCs under four different judges. It is interesting to note that while Australia allows Rough/Smooth matings, New Zealand regards the Rough and Smooth as two separate breeds and prohibits this type of mating. Australia is now affiliated to the FCI.

JUDGING THE COLLIE
The first thing I look for when judging the Collie, Rough or Smooth, is an overall balance. I am not influenced by dog or bitch that has a nice head, although for this particular breed the correct head is important. I always approach the dog in a quiet manner; it is important not to overawe a dog by looming over it. I examine the head and teeth first, and then lift the ears to see if they have been tampered with in any way, such as being held in place with sticky plaster or greased to make the fold appear more natural. I then go over the whole dog in a gentle manner. I first assess the neck for its length and arch, and then feel the placement of shoulders. I run my hands over the length of back and feel for muscle tone in the second thigh, and check for a good bend of stifle and strength of hocks. The Rough Collie is hidden under a wealth of coat, so you must feel for the bone structure and muscle tone that is so easy to see on a Smooth. It is most important to check the feet, and I do this by lifting up the paw to see shape and depth of the pad.

Next, I feel for texture of coat. I would always penalise a soft coat in a Rough Collie; the coat must be straight and fitting the lines of the body – it must never be curly. I then assess the quality of coat colour. In the tricolour I look for a gleaming black colour, with no hint of rust in the black part, good, rich tan markings, and the white markings must be clean and sparkling. When I am judging the blue merle, my preference is for a clear silvery-blue with no heavy patches of black, and I never like to see a rusty tinge in body coat. I like to see good head markings on a blue merle, and, for me, an added bonus is a small white blaze breaking up an otherwise plain head. Although sable means any colour from pale gold to rich mahogany, I prefer to see a rich golden sable with full white collar, as the sable without these markings can be so easily overlooked among the striking colours of the blue merle or tricolour. I know of one beautiful sable bitch, Crossfells Blissfull, who waited almost five years to take her title, and I am sure this was only due to the colour being less fashionable, as she was a really outstanding bitch.

After 'going over' the Collie, I ask the handler to move the Collie firstly in a triangle and then straight up and down. This shows me the hind movement as the dog moves away, the side action, and finally the front action as the dog comes towards me. If I am doubtful about any aspect of the movement, I will ask the handler to move straight down the ring and back, one more time. While the dog is moving I look for a correctly carried tail, as I would personally penalise a Collie, Rough or Smooth, that carries its tail over its back – not only does it look unsightly, it spoils the whole outline of the Collie.

The movement of the Collie, Rough and Smooth, should be free, light, and graceful. When the dog is walking, the action should be low and springy, but when striding out the dog should have good reach in the forequarters and strong driving power in the hindquarters. A sound-moving

International judge Harry McLaren judging his favourite breed.

Collie, covering the ground well, is a joy to watch; and, for me, one of the pleasures in life is to see a well-presented Collie of correct proportions, standing and showing its many virtues.

When I am judging, I am positive in my placing and confident in my manner. There is nothing worse than an indecisive judge, wandering aimlessly around the ring, taking far too long in choosing the winners; this is most unsettling for dogs and handlers alike. I am always polite to my exhibitors, knowing that they have honoured me with their entries and given me the pleasure of going over their dogs.

I always explain to my ring steward exactly how I want my ring organised; the steward's role is to assist the judge and ensure that everyone knows what is happening. I always wear something smart, but comfortable. I would never wear anything bright or flowing – and sensible shoes are a must. It is important to remember that you have been invited to judge, and this is an honour. A smart, well-turned-out judge, doing a good job in the ring, is a bonus for any show committee.

I have never come across an aggressive Collie, but if the situation arose, I would first ask the owner to assist by holding the dog's head steady. In this way, I would still be able to assess the dog, but safely. If the owner was unwilling to do this for me, and the dog was still very aggressive, then I would be left with no option but to send the dog out of the ring, explaining my actions to the steward.

If I am judging a big class, I select at least ten of the best specimens on view, and from these final dogs I will choose my class winner. At the end of the last class I will choose the best dog, who will then challenge the best bitch for Best of Breed. When judging a Rough Collie you must always send in the very best exhibit to the Group, for the Group judge will not be a breed specialist, but will probably be a working breed all-round judge. That is why it is so important to send in a really sound Rough Collie – one that not only looks beautiful, but one that can also move well. An all-round judge likes a leg on each corner, and will be very critical of movement. Not all judges look for the same things; some spend more time looking for a big coat, or a small eye, or a special colour. However, it is the overall balance of the dog that should be the first priority.

When you are judging, you must always have the confidence to judge without fear or favour. If your friend has the best dog, put it up. Equally, if your friend has a bad dog, put it down – never ever do favours in the ring. If the best dog is one you have bred, put it up; you will only look a fool if you are the only judge not to place that particular dog. Never be afraid to give your verdict, and always explain fully to any exhibitor who wishes to know why you did not place their dog. Remember the exhibitors have paid for your opinion, and if someone asks for it, once judging has been concluded, you should be willing to cooperate. Never be too harsh in your judgement; just explain kindly the reasons for your selections.

JUDGING ABROAD

I have been very fortunate in my judging career to have been invited to judge in many countries, including Finland, Spain, Italy, Hungary, Austria, Sweden and Luxemburg, and I have enjoyed the most fantastic hospitality. It is customary for the host committee to hold a banquet the night before a show for all the overseas judges, and I can recall many splendid occasions, despite the language difficulties!

However, judging overseas often entails a lot of hard work, and I have often had as many as eighty dogs to judge, and this entails a critique on each and every dog. In these situations you have to rely on an interpreter, which can bring its own problems, as literal translations can unwittingly cause offence! As the class is assembled I go over each dog, with the interpreter explaining each point of the dog as I go over it. The interpreter must then translate my verbal opinions for the written critique.

I have now owned dogs for over twenty-five years; I showed my first Collie (Rough) in 1968, and my first judging appointment was in 1971, but I can still say that I learn something new every time I enter the show ring. I believe it is important to retain this enthusiasm, and to be prepared to learn from every new experience. Judging must be a matter of personal opinion, no matter how closely you follow the Breed Standard; so it is important never to condemn a dog outright – for all you know, the very next judge that examines it will find all the points that they consider desirable in the breed!

Chapter Eleven

THE VERSATILE COLLIE

The working ability of both the Rough and the Smooth Collie has not really been exploited in Britain since the time when both breeds were used by farmers for herding and driving stock. The Rough Collie was formerly used as a Highland dog, directing and finding big flocks high up in the rugged cold mountains. The Smooth Collie was used as a lowlander dog, and was employed to drive the flocks to market. The Smooth Collie also had a reputation as a war dog, carrying messages through difficult country under fire, and tracking back behind the lines. The instinct and ability is still present in the Rough and the Smooth Collie. There are a few Rough Collies, and a higher number of Smooth Collies, who still work with sheep and cattle and are excellent at their work. The Smooth Collie will make an excellent sheepdog, but it really comes into its own when it is used to work cattle. I was lucky enough to see Int. Ch. Astrellita Blue Macho working a herd of cattle in the high meadows in Switzerland. It was a great joy to see this beautiful well-made Smooth Collie doing the work he was bred to do. Macho works hard all the week for Willie Chappui, and then returns home at weekends to be shown at all the major shows on the Continent by Gerald Martin. Gerald and Willie bred the first litter of Smooth Collies in Switzerland for twenty-six years and have done much to promote the breed in their own country.

My own Ch. Astrellita Moonstone was another outstanding example of the work capabilities of these very special dogs. She was sold at ten weeks to a farmer in Suffolk to work his cattle, and she did an excellent job herding the cows and bringing them in for milking. When the owners sold up to go abroad to open a riding stables, they asked if I would like to have the bitch back. As I had bred her, I felt responsible for her, and so I went along to collect her the following week. When I first saw her, I was amazed at her quality and condition. She was in such perfect condition that I promptly entered her for the Smooth Collie club show. This bitch had lived on a farm all her life; she had never worn a collar or walked on a lead, or been anywhere away from the farm. However, she walked into the ring as if she had been a show bitch all her life. I had no idea how she would react in that different environment, but she charmed everyone with her poise and showmanship to take Best of Breed Smooth, and Reserve Best in Show. She then went on to win five consecutive CCs, and so gained her title of Champion in just two and a half weeks. After winning her fifth CC we retired her from the show ring to enjoy life as a family companion and brood bitch. This is just another example of the way the Smooth Collie can adapt to a different environment and it also proves that this breed can be equally good at work and show.

TEMPERAMENT TESTS

In Britain and America there are no temperament tests for any of the breeds in the Working Group,

Am. Ch. Call-Me Winning Colors HC working sheep.

Int. Ch. Astrellita Blue Macho working cattle at his home in Switzerland.

A study in concentration: Lancelot Black Bryony, Foxearth Minnie Alopex and Aunt Gillespie Alopex prepare to do the retrieve with their dumb-bells. All three are owned and trained by Tony and Isobel Griffiths.   *Alopex.*

Trained Rough Collies in Italy, bred by Aileen Speding.

but in Europe the working ability and temperament of the two Collie breeds is most important. In Sweden, for example, no dog in the Working Group can become a full Champion until it has passed a temperament test. The idea of this test is to make sure that any dog that bears the title of Champion should be of sound mind and temperament, especially as it will probably be bred from. Each dog is trained beforehand, and is well prepared for the work involved.

Lyn Westby, a British judge, was invited to watch one of these tests in progress, as they were held on the same day as the International Championship show. The dog she saw being tested was the Smooth Collie Ch. Fairlines First Class Maid. Mrs Westby writes:

"The test took place in thick forest behind the showground. The dog is first walked on a lead with its owner along a woodland path. After a few hundred yards the dog is confronted, at some distance away, by a figure disguised at that moment by a coat or something over his head. The dog may start or even bark, but it must not attempt to run away. As the person approaches, he slowly removes his disguise and by the time he is near the dog, he is just a stranger approaching. The dog must not show any aggression. It is not expected to be over-friendly, but it must not back away. The dog must allow the person to walk past, just as it would be expected to do in any street.

"Continuing along the path, a gun is fired at a distance, and again the dog may well start and look surprised, but it must not show any aggression or real fear. The idea was that the dog could tolerate loud, unexpected noises such as a car backfiring, without becoming unnerved. The dog was then asked to walk past some loud clanging chains and old tins banging together, to prove it would not be startled by loud noises such as roadworks and trains.

"The dog must then walk over a narrow bridge and through some barriers, all of which could be encountered in any street. At all times, the dog must show confidence in its handler, and be sufficiently good-natured to live a normal happy life, as a show dog or as a family pet. When a dog has passed this test it has proved that it can be an asset to the breed, and that a dog with a sound mind is a pleasure to live with."

OBEDIENCE
Most Collies, Rough or Smooth, can be trained to compete in Obedience and Agility. The Collie has the instinct to work, and the majority enjoy the stimulation of special training. In the UK many Smooth Collie owners are involved in this side of dog-owning, but not so many Rough Collie owners. Tony and Isobel Griffiths have a wonderful time with their Smooths, competing in Obedience contests and in the show ring. Mrs Jan Starkey and her family are very active owners, not only competing in Agility and Obedience with their dogs, but they can also be seen regularly in the show ring. They are the owners of the tricolour bitch Ch. Newarp Dark Midnight.

AMERICA
In America more owners get involved with Obedience training, and both Rough and Smooth Collies are worked to high honours. In the US an Obedience degree is awarded when a dog has earned three qualifying scores at an American Kennel Club licensed show under three different judges. A qualifying score is a total of 170 points, and over fifty per cent of these points must be earned with each exercise.

CD after a dog's name means that the dog is classed as a Companion Dog. This test requires the dog to heel on and off the lead, recall, stand to be examined, respond to the commands sit, and down and stay.

CDX refers to Companion Dog Excellent, and this involves a more difficult version of the CD test, plus jumping over hurdles, retrieving, and dropping down on recall when the handler is out of sight. A Collie must be able to jump one and a half times the height at his shoulders for a high jump, and three times that height for a broad jump.

UD The Utility Dog degree is much harder, as this requires the dog to pick out an article with its owner's smell on it from a group of identical but unscented objects. The dog must follow signals to jump, retrieve and stand. During these exercises handlers are not allowed to touch their dogs.

TD The Tracking Dog title is for those interested in training their dogs in a more specialised skill. To obtain the title of TD, a dog must find an article dropped at the end of a track about 500 yards in length. This track must have at least two turns in it, and the test must take no more than two hours.

The American Kennel Club award an Obedience Trial Champion certificate (OT Ch.) and this award is given when a dog has obtained 100 points in Obedience competitions, including three first prizes in each group. Only a few Collies have won this title. The first was Ch. & OT Ch. Shoreham Dubious Delight UDT, a Rough tricolour male, owned and trained by Jennifer Julander from California, and he won his title in 1974. Another Rough Collie to win this title was OT Ch. Walstone Impulse, a tricolour bitch owned by Madeline Loos of New Jersey, and in 1975 the title was won by Ch. OT Ch. North Country Wildfire UD, a sable and white Rough Collie, owned and trained by Sandra Hall.

In 1957 a Smooth Collie, Ch. Shamrock Smooth Rocket UD, was the first Champion to gain the UD award. He sired a stream of winners including four CD dogs, who were trained to help blind children. The Shamrock Smooth Collies produced many Obedience dogs and eighteen became Champions. Over thirty Smooth Collies became guide dogs for the blind, proving once again the ability of a Smooth Collie to use its working brain to the full.

Many kennels have no wish to enter their Collies at a beauty competition, but they get much satisfaction in training their Collies to be obedience and tracking dogs. Inga Holm and her daughter, Lily Mattesky, of Fort Lauderdale, Florida have trained three dogs to their titles. Other great names on the American Obedience scene are Jan Shields of California and Carol Knock of Ohio, who have both trained many Collies to their titles.

DENMARK

In Denmark there are two different kinds of obedience work. One type is working classes, which is like police-dog work and is most popular with breeds such as the German Shepherd and the Dobermann. Rough Collies are better suited to the ordinary Obedience classes, which entail heelwork, sit, down, recall, jump, distance control, send away and scent discrimination. These exercises are divided into four Obedience classes, graduating with increasing difficulty. The classes are numbered from 1 to 4, with class 4 as the most difficult class.

Marianne Dellinger has enjoyed great success in Obedience competitions with her Rough Collie, Qualibet's Mr Rames (also known as Rocky). He made breed history by becoming the first Rough Collie Obedience Champion in Denmark, in 1985. Marianne tells Rocky's story in her own words: "I first started training Rocky because I think that if one has a dog it is important to have a well-behaved dog. I also chose to train Rocky because I knew that Collies were intelligent animals, based on what I had heard about their work as shepherd dogs, and their use in filming *Lassie*. I guess I was also fascinated by the challenge of communication between man and animal.

"We started training in the Danish class 1 (beginners), and our instructor encouraged us to try for the class 1 competitions. After just a short time, we were winning at this level, and people started to encourage us to try for class 2. The level of difficulty was, of course, greater, but again, after a short time, Rocky started to win and again people started to encourage us to continue to the next

Dk. Ch. Qualibets Black Mr Herman: won his Obedience title at the age of five years.

level. For class 3, I changed my strategy. I did a lot of the training myself, and I supplemented it with training at the local Police Dog Club. So at the time, we were training for two difficult, but quite different programmes, namely class 3 and police dog training. We won competitions at the Police Dog Club, and it surprised the experienced dog handlers with their big and strong German Shepherds that a young girl and her Collie could beat them at their own specialty.

"We now started focusing on my dream to obtain the Obedience Championship. This was our most successful period in my dog-training career as we continued to compete at the Police Dog Club and started to win class 3 with very high scores. In 1985, the dream came true – Rocky and I obtained the Obedience Championship. As Rocky was the first Rough Collie to win this title, the dog magazines and the local papers wrote a lot about Rocky and my other dog, Ruffas, a Samoyed that was winning quite a few show competitions.

"Some years later, another Collie, Qualibet's Black Mr Herman, won the Danish Obedience Championship. He was related to Rocky as they both had a common ancestor. Rocky is still a beautiful and intelligent dog, who is taking it easy in retirement from the competition circuits. If it hadn't have been for an undescended testicle, which by Danish Rules kept him from competing in show competitions, I am sure that I would have had him competing in that area too."

TRACKING AND RESCUE WORK
Int. Ch. Perterblue Harvey gained fame not only as an International Champion in the show ring,

*Int. Ch. Peterblue Harvey: awarded the gold
medal for his work as a rescue dog in Switzerland.*

but was also awarded the gold medal for his work as a rescue dog. He was bred by the Peterblue
kennels, and was proudly owned by Miss Meyer in Switzerland.

Collie specialist Lyn Westby relates how Ch. Fairlines First Class Maid, having passed her
temperament test in Sweden, was invited with her owner, Margaretta Andersson, to see how she
would take to tracking and rescue work. Many breeds compete in these tests in Sweden, and
Kirsten and Don Birminge have some of the top trial Rough Collies in this sphere.

They drove to the thickly forested area near Kinra to put the Smooth Collie to the test, and as
this bitch lives in a town she had never experienced this sort of environment. They watched for a
while as Mr Birminge played with the dogs with some small off-cuts of wood, and then he set off
into the forest with the dogs, leaving six pieces of wood hidden in six different places. A tricolour
bitch, still in the process of being trained for competition, was sent to track his trail and fetch back
the wooden pieces one by one. No guidance was given at any time; she had to search with her nose
entirely. A great fuss was made of her each time she returned with her prize.

The ultimate test is to find people who are lost in the vast forests – this is a situation that occurs
in severe snow conditions in the long winter months. A sable Rough Collie, who is a top search
dog in Sweden, made this look easy, putting his nose down and following his master's scent to the
different places he had left the 'body'. The Smooth bitch was then given a try. She was not going
to be asked to find the wood pieces, as first she had to be taught to retrieve. Her owner was sent
some distance into the forest, completely out of sight, and then the bitch was taken on a tracking
harness to the start, and encouraged to get her nose down and sniff where her owner had gone. She
sniffed the ground and then put her head up to sniff the air, but Kirsten directed her down again.
Suddenly she got the scent and was off, zig zagging through the trees, tracking her mistress. She

Mary Court, winner of the Treetops Shield in 1989, with her Rough Collie, Elvaston Royal Scott.

lifted her head once or twice, and again she was encouraged to follow the scent trail. She eventually found her quarry behind a tree – to the great excitement of all concerned.

The same thing was tried again in a different part of the forest, and with Kirsten giving encouragement, and slight guidance each time she lifted her head away from the ground scent, she again found her owner, with much barking and tail-wagging. According to Lyn, it was a wonderful experience see a Collie tracking some distance into the forest at her first attempt, proving the ability of Smooth Collies to work and to be of use.

JUNIOR HANDLING

One young lady who has had great success in the ring is Mary Court, a very talented young handler, who has won the Treetops Trophy, awarded to the best junior handler for three years in succession. In order to win this coveted prize it is essential to have a steady dog, with a superb temperament. The dog Mary shows is her own Rough Collie, Elvaston Royal Scott, and together they won the award for gaining the most points in the year. Mary is under twelve years old, and so this is an excellent record. 'Scott' thoroughly enjoys the limelight, and is proof that if a Rough Collie is given a job of work to do, it is more than ready to oblige.

SHOW BUSINESS
LASSIE
In 1940 Eric Knight wrote the classic book *Lassie Come Home,* and when Metro Goldwyn Meyer decided to make a film of the book the Rough Collie became an international star. Eight Lassie films were made, with stars such as Elizabeth Taylor and Roddy McDowell attempting to grab the limelight from Lassie. In fact, the first Lassie was chosen by sheer chance. Filming was due to start when it was found that the lovely Collie bitch, who had been trained to play the part of Lassie, had dropped her coat and was near naked. Rudd Weatherwax, an established dog trainer, was alerted, but the only Collie he had was a male, named Pal. However, Pal got the part, and from that time onwards Lassie has always been played by a male. Pal made six films, the last in 1951. In 1954 it was decided that Lassie should be made into a television series, and although Pal was retired, his descendants carried on where he left off. A total of 589 original episodes of *Lassie* have been made over the years, thrilling many a young collie lover to this day.

MOTHER GOOSE
The Rough Collie Ch. Jefsfire Tudor Queen, owned by Mr and Mrs A. Jeffries, was given a walk-on part in the Christmas Pantomime *Mother Goose,* starring the well-known singer Frank Ifield. Tudor Queen, who was three years old at the time, was asked to step in at short notice, as two predecessors – both cross-breeds – had been dismissed for biting during rehearsals!

Tudor Queen had to walk on stage and give a kiss to a sleeping shepherd girl. She did this faultlessly, twice daily for six weeks. She was collected by taxi every day, and taken backstage to a kennel where she stayed between shows. The hectic goings-on around her went unnoticed; she always knew what was needed of her, and she took a bow when the audience applauded at the end of the show. In fact, she spent most of her time in Frank Ifield's dressing room, and often went out shopping with Beryl Reid, who was also in the show.

On one occasion someone left her kennel door undone, and she appeared on the stage when not required. Ted Rogers, who was on stage at the time, ad libbed saying "The ladies is over there," and off she trotted, to much applause!

THE SUNNYBANK COLLIES
Albert Payson Terhune, wrote *His Mate*, published in 1915, which was all about his Rough Collie, Lad, one of his many Sunnybank Collies. His next book, *Lad: A Dog,* was published in a limited edition selling for just $2.00, and by 1922 the book was a best-seller. This was no overnight success: the book kept on selling and selling, and by 1975 it had sold over 250,000 copies. Mr Terhune wrote over twenty books, and he also gave a weekly talk on the radio from 1934 to 1936, giving advice to dog owners. He showed his Collies for a short time and he also judged. He died in 1942 and after his wife's death the Sunnybank estate, which was set in many acres, was opened to the public as a park. It is at this park that the Collie Club of Northern New Jersey hold their show, and the Sunnybank Memorial Festival is held there each year.

Chapter Twelve

COLLIES IN NORTH AMERICA

One of the very first imports was a Rough Collie bred by Mr Mercier in Ireland, sired by The Colonel out of a bitch called Jessie. The dog was named Ch. Dublin Scot – he gained his title in 1887. Scot sired many good Collies. His son, Ch. Scotilla, went on to sire Ch. Roslyn Wiles, born in 1889, who gained the title in 1892. Scot and Scotilla were owned by the Chestnut Hill kennels, which imported many English Collies to help swell the gene pool. Some excellent stock was imported from Scotland in those days, and breeders such as Mr J. Agnew, Mr R. Tait and Mr J. Dalgleish were responsible for many of the early American Rough Collies. In 1890 Mr W. Arkwright sent over his lovely top winning blue merle bitch, Ch. Blue Ruin, who was said to be one of the best coloured blues of all time.

From then on there was a steady flow of Rough Collies across the Atlantic, and from these early imports the Rough Collie has emerged as one of North America's most popular breeds. Mr W. Stansfield, already famous for his excellent Collies, sent over many top quality Collies, carrying the Laund prefix. The famous Bellhaven kennels were founded on lines from Laund breeding. Mrs Florence B. Ilch, of New Jersey, imported Ch. Laund Liberation, who made a lasting impression on the breed by winning sixty-five Best of Breed awards. Among her other imports were Am. Eng. Ch. Laund Lector of Bellhaven, Ch. Laund Logic, and the outstanding sable and white Laund Loyalty of Bellhaven, who at the tender age of nine months went Best in Show at the 1929 Westminster Show – his first and only outing in the show ring. It was the first time a Rough Collie had ever won that award.

By the end of the 1920s Mrs Ilch had bred eighteen Champions and imported eleven others who also gained their titles. Her English import Ch. Laund Limit was the sire of both Ch. Bellhaven Laund Logic and Ch. Alstead Laund Luminous. Another of Mrs Ilch's imports was the outstanding sire Ch. Lucason of Ashtead O'Bellhaven, born in 1928 and bred by Mr R. W. Roberts in England; he gained his title in 1930. Lucason sired Ch. Bellhaven Black Lucason, who in turn sired Ch. Bellhaven Standard Bearer, who went on to sire Ch. Bellhaven Gold Standard. From the photos, it can be seen that these were beautiful dogs of outstanding quality. The Bellhaven kennels bred a grand total of ninety Champions – a record that must be unbeatable. The last Bellhaven Champion was Ch. Heathfield Lance O'Bellhaven, who was made up in 1960.

Mrs Lunt was to import many of England's top studs, and was a leading breeder of Collies until her death in late 1950. Her prefix, Alstead, appeared on many pedigrees. Ch. Alstead Laund Luminous, a son of Ch. Laund Limit proved to be a great asset to Mrs Lunt's kennels. Mrs Lunt imported a son of Ch. Magnet, bred by John R. Morley in England. His name was Eng. Ch. Alstead Seedley Supremacy, and he was born in 1919. He was the sire of three Champions to three

Four generations of Champions, bred by Florence Ilch (pictured left to right): Triple Ch. Lucason of Ashtead O'Bellhaven (Lucas of Ashtead – Jean of Ashtead, 1928), Ch. Bellhaven Black Lucason (Triple Ch. Lucason of Ashtead O'Bellhaven – Ch. Viola of Ashtead O'Bellhaven, 1931), Ch. Bellhaven Standard Bearer (Ch. Bellhaven Black Lucason – Ch. Bellhaven Lady Lector, 1933), and Ch. Bellhaven Gold Standard (Ch. Bellhaven Standard Bearer – Ch. Eden Edith of Bellhaven, 1935).

different bitches. Magnet himself was imported as a much older dog, having proved himself in England by siring Eng. Ch. Poplar Perfection. Magnet was reputedly purchased for his beautiful head qualities and sweet expression, and he also carried a profuse coat. Mrs Ilch purchased the sable and white Ch. Starbat Strongheart, born in 1920 and sired by Eng. Ch. Alstead Laund Luminous. He was a well-made dog, with profuse coat and excellent neck. He was well-used at stud, and was one of America's biggest home-bred winners of that era. He produced, among others, Ch. Bellhaven Stronghold and Ch. Bellhaven Bigheart, who was the grandsire of Ch. El Troubadour of Arken.

An English import of great significance was Eden Emerald, born in 1922, later to become Ch. Alstead Eden Emerald. He was a grandson of Ch. Magnet on his sire's side, and his dam was a maternal grand-daughter of Ch. Laund Limit, and by blending these two famous lines together, the strong lines that still exist today were produced. At least eighty per cent of modern American Collies are descended from these lines.

The thirties saw the start of the great depression, and fewer Collies were registered. Many of the bigger kennels were able to continue breeding, and one dog to make his mark as a prolific producer was Ch. El Troubadour of Arken, who sired a total of fifteen Champions. When mated to his kennel mate, Ch. Nymph of Arken, he sired his most famous litter which included: Ch. Future of Arken, Ch. Cock Robin of Arken and Ch. A Glow of Arken. Troubadour was only fifteen

Earl Of Narragansette, a son of Ch. Forth of Narragansette, bred by Harry McLaren in England, leaving for Kansas.

*Cowper.
Photo Courtesy
H. McLaren.*

months old at the time, and this was the start of a most successful stud career. Ch. Future of Arken was Troubadour's most famous son – he sired five Champions in one year, 1934 .

It would be impossible to name all the imports that made their way to the USA, but Collies from the Parbold, Seedley, Southport, Wishaw and the Ormskirk kennels all played their part in the development of the breed. In the early thirties Mrs N. George, of the Beulahs prefix, sent many a good winner over. Ch. Beulahs Silver The Merrik was born in 1934, and gained his USA title in 1937. He was followed by Ch. Beulahs Golden Sultan, who gained his title in 1940. Many years ago I remember walking my dogs in a London park, and a young lady came over and asked what type of Collies they were. When I told her that they were Rough Collies, she replied, with great dignity: "I have Collies, but mine are Beulahs Collies!" Such was the fame of this prefix.

The late 1930s and early 1940s saw the American scene surge with good home-bred stock, and this was a good thing, as due to the Second World War imports came to a standstill and America had to make good use of the breeding stock already in the top kennels. The Rough Collie in America was becoming more widespread, with kennels of top show Collies, such as the Noranda Collies in New York; and in Oklahoma Mrs Florence Cummings bred many Champions carrying her Arrowhill prefix and made a significant contribution to the development of the Rough Collie in America. With her husband, she bred many beautiful Champions, and they were founders of the first Collie Club in Oklahoma. The influence that this kennel had on the breed came from their

Ch. Bririch Gold Emblem, aged eight years. This dog, bred by Vera Hickson of the famous Bririch kennels, was the first post-war Champion import to the USA.

Am. Ch. Silva Cymbal from Shiel (Ch. Westcarrs Blue Minoru – Silva Seabear from Shiel) won a CC in the UK at eight months and was then sold to the USA.

outstanding stud dogs: Arrowhill Ace High sired sixteen Champions, Ch. Arrowhill Oklahoma Man sired eleven Champions, and the sire to make history was Ch. High Man of Arrowhill. This dog was the sire of six Champions, including the world-famous Ch. Black Hawk of Kasan, the outstanding Smooth Collie who took the show scene by storm and became the first Smooth Collie to win a Best in Show award in the USA.

Ch. Silver Ho Parader was one of America's most prolific stud dogs, siring thirty-seven Champions. Among the many top winning Parader Champions were: Ch. Paraders Golden Image

(1945), Ch. Paraders Bold Venture (1950), Ch. Paraders Country Squire (1958), and Ch. Paraders Reflection (1966). Ch. Parader Bold Venture won at the Collie Club of America in 1955 and 1957, and he also produced twenty-four Champions. His son, Ch Paraders Country Squire, also sired twenty-four Champions, including Ch. Paraders Reflection, who sired seventeen Champions. Among Squire's Champion offspring was Ch. Two Jays Hanover Enterprise, who sired forty-five Rough Collie Champions. Many of today's kennels carry these important bloodlines.

Another very important kennel was owned by Dr James H. Mangels Jr. Based in Connecticut, the Gaylord Collies soon became well-known, producing some outstanding winners, such as Ch. Gaylord Mr Scalawag. Later, in Long Island, Trudy Mangels founded her famous Brandwyne kennels, and with careful line breeding produced beautiful Collies, true to type. Her Ch. Brandwyne Destiny's Echo produced twenty-three Champions, including one Smooth. Many of today's kennels owe a great deal to these dedicated breeders who worked so hard, and at great expense, to make the Collie great in America. I believe that the Americans have kept the Collie true to type, and they have produced some outstanding stock. The American breeders and handlers present their Collies in the most fantastic condition, and they are groomed to perfection.

THE COLLIE CLUB OF AMERICA
The American Kennel Club was established in 1884, and the Collie Club of America was formed in New York City on August 26th 1886. The first president was Mr Jenkins Van Schaick, who held office until he died in 1889. The Collie Club of America was the first Collie club to be a member of the American Kennel Club and was deemed to be Parent club. In 1908 the Collie Club of America voted that Smooth Collies should compete on equal terms with Rough Collies, and in 1912 new rules were drawn up expanding the club to include all parts of the USA and Canada. By 1947 there were over 1,000 members, and many local clubs had been formed. In 1956 the Illustrated Standard for Collies was printed, with superb artwork by Mrs Lorraine A. Still, and this has become a classic for Collie owners all over the world.

THE SMOOTH COLLIE
Smooth Collies were shown as early as 1880 in the USA, and there are records of Smooths being shown at the prestigious Westminster Show in 1888. By the early 1900s Smooth Collies were shown on a more regular basis, and in 1906 a Smooth bitch, exported by Tom Stretch, gained her title to become Ch. Ormskirk Mabel, followed in 1907 by her daughter, Ch. Ormskirk Lucy. In these early days the Smooth Collie failed to reach the heights of popularity of the more glamorous Rough Collie. Classes were dropped, and very few Smooths were seen around the shows. During the years 1915 to 1923 a few Smooth Collies were shown, but no Champions were made up, and so the American Smooth Collie did not really establish itself until the 1940s.

However, the breed benifited from some of the early imports. These included the Laund Collies, bred by Mr Stansfield, and from these imports came the well-known Pebble Ledge kennels, owned by Margaret Haserot, who laid the foundation for the Smooth Collies in America. In 1953 Solo from Shiel was imported from the famous kennels of Miss Margaret Osborne, who also sent over Sparrow from Shiel and Silvacymbil from Shiel. Solo from Shiel was a highly influential dam, producing winning offspring from all her litters. In her first litter, sired by Ch. Hertzville Hightop, she produced Ch. Glengyle Smooth Sailing. In her second litter, by Mery Count of Glen Hill, she produced Ch. Glengyle Smooth Character, and in her third litter, sired by Ch. San Lori Citation, she produced Ch. Glengyle Smooth N Lovely and Ch. Glengyle Smooth Fellow.

Records show that Ch. Hertzville Hightop was a tricolour Rough Collie, and many of today's top

The famous Am. Ch. Black Hawk of Kasan, who had a major influence on the breed in the USA.

Ch. Jolee's Timbrleaf Smooth Sail'n: a typical American Smooth Collie with an elegant head, soft expression, good ear carriage and a lovely rounded muzzle – a tricolour of distinction.

kennels in America can trace their stock back to the Shiel kennels. Around this time Mrs Joan Hill of the Selskars kennels, Mrs Bishop (Laund) and Mrs R. Alexander (Peterblues) made a major impact on the breeding of Smooth Collies in the USA. Three English imports had an important influence on Smooth Collies in the United States in the breed's formative years. They were Hewburn Hallmark, Laund Blue Peter, and Laund Lofty Girl. Hallmark won Best of Breed in 1941, beating Rough Collies, and was runner-up in the Working Group. Laund Blue Peter and Laund Lofty Girl were imported by a syndicate based in California, which consisted of Mrs Lunt (Alstead), Hal Lounsbury (Halmaric), Arthur Foff (Tamalgate), Bob Willis (Alloway), and Genevieve Eames (Torryea). This group of Collie lovers shared out the resultant litters of these imports. One of these dogs went to Mr Lounsbury, and was named Halmaric Baronet. When Baronet was mated to Pebble Ledge Little Dorrit, owned by Margaret Haserot, the litter included a tricolour bitch, named Halmaric Trilby. This bitch earned her place in history by becoming the dam of the first Smooth Collie Champion in the USA for thirty-five years, and this was Ch. Pebble Ledge Bambi.

Margaret Haserot was determined to breed outstanding Smooth Collies, and although she was beset by many setbacks, she persevered to overcome her ill fortunes. She achieved her dream when she imported Ch. Laund Laventer, a blue merle, from the Laund kennels in England, and he was the sire of Pebble Lodge Little Dorrit. When Ch. Pebble Lodge Bambi was mated to the sable and white Rough Collie, Ch. Harlines Son of Cainbrooke, she produced Ch. Christopher of Pebble Ledge, the Smooth Collie who went on to sire Ch. Belle Mount Bambi. Today's breeders are indebted to these early Smooths, for they were the foundation stock of the American Smooth Collie.

The Shamrock Smooths of the early 1960s came mainly from Margaret Osborne's Shiel kennels, and were well-known for their excellent Obedience work. In these early days the Smooth Collie was looked upon as the poor relation of the glamorous Rough Collie, which was being shown and taking top awards. But this was all to change when Ch. Black Hawk of Kasan made his debut in the show ring. This outstanding tricolour was bred by Mr and Mrs Singer, and he was to have a major impact on the breed in America. Hawk was sired by the Rough Collie, Ch. High Man of Arrowhill, and his dam was Ch. Kasans Fine and Fancy. He was born on May 13th 1966, and gained his title in his first year without ever being beaten. He was the first Smooth Collie in the United States to go Best in Show at an All Breeds Show, which he did in 1970. In this year he was also the top working sire, siring fifteen Champions. He went on to sire eighty-one Champions – surely a record for all time? When he was mated to Ch. Cul Mor's Birkenshaw the result was: Ch. Chan el Sleek Tempest O'Jagwyn, owned by Elinor Pettis; Ch. Jagwyn Black Fashion and Ch. Jagwyn Mood Indigo, owned by Margaret Ulman; Ch. Jagwyn Dutch Master, owned by Barbara Teichman; and Ginny Holz's Ch. Cul Mor's Maltese Falcon and Ch. Cul Mor's Daike Wicker – what a litter! It was so successful that the mating was repeated in 1972, and this union produced four Champions: Ch. Jagwyn Shadow of the Hawk, Ch. Roydons Miss Amanda O'Jagwyn, Ch. Tossawi of Jagwyn, and Ch. Jagwyn Blue Raudi. It is interesting to note that Ch. Black Hawk of Kasan is grandfather and great-grandfather of Kel Bonnie Chan el Gina, the bitch that Christine Leach imported to Britain in order to bring back some of the lost bloodlines and to enhance the Smooth Collie in its country of origin. Gina was mated to another grandson of Hawk, Canadian Ch. Goliath O'Darjoro, and she whelped in quarantine soon after her arrival in UK. So the breed has turned full circle – from Britain to America and back again – and Ch. Black Hawk of Kasan lives on in almost every Smooth pedigree throughout the world.

Some of the modern Smooth Collie breeders owe a great debt to the early stalwarts of the breed, as the Smooth Collie was never as popular as the Rough Collie in the United States. However, the Smooth is now far more widely recognised, and it has a bigger following in the USA than in any other country in the world. There are a number of highly successful Smooth kennels in the United States, all helping to promote and develop the breed. Vern and Lora Esch founded their Verlor kennels in 1970; Maureen Burrell of the Braemar Smooth Collies started her kennels with a dog from Mr and Mrs Pettis of the Chan el kennels, and she has gone on to breed many outstanding Smooth Collie Champions. Pat Lessard, of the famous Storm Collies, used Ch. Black Hawk of Kasan to influence her line; and Mr and Mrs Leonard's Lisara kennels are responsible for many Smooth Collie Champions. They bred Ch. Lisara Morning After, who won the title of Top Smooth Collie in 1986 after winning nine Best in Show awards. Many of the Lisara bred Smooths are descendants of Ch. Black Hawk of Kasan.

To bring the Smooth Collie American scene up to date, mention must go to the exciting kennels of Maureen Camilli of the Call Me Collies. She bred Rough Collies for twenty years, and then fell in love with her first Smooth Collie some ten years ago, and has been besotted with Smooths ever since. Her first Smooth was Shadyhills Call Me Lacey, and she was the dam of Maureen's first Smooth Collie Champion, Call Me Spirit of Excellence ('Rocky'), who gained his title at the age

Am. Can. Ch. Call-Me Sunday Silence: Best of Breed at the Monroe Kennel Club, 1990.

of thirteen months. Maureen breeds Rough Collies along with her Smooths and says they complement each other very well.

Smooth Collies in Canada go back a long way, and some good Smooth-coated Collies were working cattle in the late 1800s. They were not registered with the Canadian Kennel Club, as they were results of Rough-Smooth matings, and the CKC classified them as separate breeds. In the 1960s this was changed to one breed, and registration was based on coat length.

In the sixties Mrs Joan Hill of the Selskars prefix sent out to Ontario two tricolour Smooths who became Can. Ch. Selskars Jet Wind, a male, and Can. Ch. Selskars Victoriana, a bitch. 'Rena', as she was known, was mated to another import, Ch. Ravensglen Peterblue Merrilina, from the Peterblue kennels, owned by Mrs Kay Alexander. The Sconestone prefix, owned by Mrs Weston, carried many lines to the Selskars Smooths, and included Selskars Mr Macduff of Sconestone CD.

The two best-known kennels of Smooth Collies in Canada belong to Maureen Burrell of the Braemar prefix, and the Mistyhaven Collies, owned by George Fedyck. Maureen Burrell owned the litter brother to Kelbonnie Chan el Gina, the Smooth bitch imported to England in the seventies by Christine Leach. Mr Fendyck's first Smooth was Am. Can. Ch. BJ's Centrefold. She had three litters, producing two American Champions. She was also the dam of Can. Ch. Mistyhavens Dark Jewel, who went on to produce Am. Ch. Scot Dales Riverboat Gambler – the Winners Dog at the 1980 Collie Club of America show. The Mistyhaven kennels have produced or owned fifty-two Champions.

Chapter Thirteen

THE COLLIE WORLDWIDE

AUSTRALIA

THE ROUGH COLLIE

It was in the 1880s that the first Rough Collies arrived in Australia, imported from England. In 1894 a meeting was held for all those interested in the Collie, and the result was the formation of the Victorian Collie Club, one of the first clubs to specialise in the breed in the country. Unfortunately the club was disbanded in 1902 and was not re-formed until 1911. The club held its first Championship show in May 1912, and one of the first Rough Collies to become a Champion was Mr W. Cockbill's Amietta Adonis. In honour of this prestigious win the dog pavilion at the Royal Melbourne Showground was named after him.

The first dog show was known as the Queensland National Exhibition – the word 'Royal' was not added until much later. There were no Collies, or Sheepdogs, at the first show in 1876. In 1880 Collies were first mentioned, and were shown as 'Sheepdogs'. In 1882 a six-year-old dog appeared in the catalogue. His name was Laird, and he was a dark sable, 20 inches in height and weighing 45lbs. His sire was Cocksie and his dam was Moss Rose. Cocksie was the son of Old Cockie, who was born in 1868 and died in 1882, and so Laird must have been one of the very early imports to Australia. In a catalogue, dated 1886, Collies classes were scheduled. Dogs listed included: Laddie, Shep, Scottie and Glen; and the bitches included: Floss, Lassie, Bessie and Trusty. In 1892 the first important imports arrived from England – Ormskirk Amazement, Ormskirk Grace, Westwood Victor, and Aberfeldie Pearl.

The Collie Club of Victoria was formed in 1931, and this club held its first show in 1933 with a total entry of fifty Collies. In 1982 the club celebrated its fiftieth anniversary, with Kath Jeffries of the well-known Jefsfire kennels officiating. This show drew a super entry of 284 Collies, including twelve Smooth Collies. The Collie Club of New South Wales was formed in 1943, and one of the founders of this club was Miss Joyce O'Reilly, who later moved to England and become the well-known Mrs Joyce Sargeant of the Carramar kennels, famous for their fabulous blue merle Collies.

In 1987 the Collie National Championship and Obedience Trial was hosted by the Collie Club of New South Wales, and the judge was Mr L. R. Peelan from Holland. The first day was for Obedience dogs and bitches, and then there were classes for all the male Collies Rough and Smooth. The following day was for bitches, plus the special classes such as Progeny, Brace, and Property classes. It was interesting to note that in the schedule it states that bitches on heat may be shown in all classes other than Obedience. I was sent a video of this show and I have never seen so many trophies given out at one show, anywhere in the world. All the Collies – Rough and Smooth

– were of outstanding quality, and the presentation and handling were fantastic. I noticed that the professional handlers changed clothes to suit the colour of the dog they were showing. I was surprised at the amount of coat the Rough Collies carried, and they were all in tip-top condition.

The Glendallo and Cathkin kennels of Glad Osborne and Gaye Jones are the most consistent winners; they have bred many Champions that could win anywhere in the world. Sydney is the home of the Kollylock Rough Collies. Aust. Ch. Kollylock My Mystic won Best in Show All Breeds at the Sydney Royal under Mr R. Vuorinen, the well-known Collie judge from Finland. The Glenallen kennels, owned by Mrs D. Allen, also has much to be proud of, breeding consistently to the Standard. Aust. Ch. Glenallen Gay Blue Danube won Best Exhibit in Group at the Melbourne Royal in 1986, and Best in Group at the Canberra Royal in 1987. Some beautiful Rough Collies have left England to grace the

Ch. and Aust. Ch. Corydon Glory
Hallelujah.   Lene Halvorsen.

show rings of Australia, including one of my favourite dogs, Ch. Little Caesar of Corydon. This dog is a magnificent shaded sable, with the most beautiful expression. He was typically male, with a superb coat, and movement that was second to none. Other Corydons to emigrate 'down under' were Ch. Corydon Quinault and Ch. Corydon Handsome Hero, winner of twelve CCs. They were soon followed by Ch. Corydon Tucks Tiger, who soon made his presence felt, winning sixteen CCs in an unbeaten run, which included nine Groups, and seven Best in Show, All Breeds – a record that will take some beating. Barry and Leah Ryan imported two outstanding Rough Collies – Rainshade Noblesse Oblige and Rains Sans Souci – from the American kennels of Dr Sharon Lynn Vanderlip. I am sure the tricolour dog, Rainshade Noblesse Oblige, will have a great future as a stud dog, and will have a great influence on the breed.

THE SMOOTH COLLIE

Smooth Collies are believed to have been established in Australia as early as the late 1890s and early 1900s, but I have no records of these early years. It is believed that a Smooth Collie was crossed with a dingo in about 1840, and the result was the Australian Cattle Dog, as it is known today.

In 1975 Janice Cook imported two Smooth Collies from England – a tricolour bitch, Foxearth Black Faith, who was sired by Foxwitchen Luke, and a blue dog, Cotsbelle Ling, who was by Eng. Ch. Jalondas Blue Apollo out of Cotsbelle True Love – and they both became Australian Champions. The Smooth Collie Association of Australasia was formed after a discussion with breeders at the Melbourne Royal Show in 1986, and it has many members. Although the Smooth Collie is a minority breed, it is well-known in the big ring taking major awards.

In Australia Smooths and Roughs may be interbred and many Champions are the result of cross matings. Lynda Garland's Catfall kennels are well-known for the Smooth Collies they show; her Aust. Ch. Celavie Body Line has been a consistent winner and an excellent stud, producing some good youngsters, all winning under specialist and all-round judges. Janice Cook's Foxbell kennels are still producing popular winners, and they have notched up some important wins. Jane Doyle left England with her Talcott Smooth Collies, and she has gone from strength to strength breeding outstanding winning Collies. While in England Jane was very fortunate in being able to buy Ralph of Talcott, one of the puppies whelped by the imported bitch, Kelbonnie Gina, owned by Christine Leach, who imported her in whelp.

In 1982 Gaye Jones of Sydney bred her first litter of Rough-Smooth puppies from the tricolour Rough dog, Cathkin After Dark, out of the Smooth bitch, Foxearth Blue Folly, who came from Janice Cook's kennels in Victoria. From this litter, a tricolour Smooth bitch was purchased by Tony and Jan Watson, breeders of

Lioja Megastar (Eng. Aust. Ch. Astrellita Midnight Dynamo – Lioja Wicked Witch).

Rough Collies since 1975. This bitch was to be the foundation of their Smooth Collies. She was named Cathkin Smooth as Silk ('Charm'), and she obtained her title at the age of ten months. She was a Group winner, a Best in Show winner, and she was Best of Breed at the Brisbane Royal National in 1983 at just seven months of age. She was mated to Ch. Aulda Dunegal Roshmede, and produced a litter of Roughs and Smooths. A sable Smooth male was kept from this litter, and he went on to become Ch. Lioja Plain Lucky. His sister, Lioja Smooth Placement, did not like shows and so did not gain her title, but she was bred from and produced Ch. Lioja Plain Copy.

I heard through a friend that Jan and Tony were looking for an English Smooth stud dog, and so arrangements were made to send out my newly-crowned Ch. Astrellita Midnight Dynamo, a young tricolour, who was a clown of a dog, with a wonderful nature, loving children, cats, and other dogs, so he was considered ideal. He was sired by Astrellita Able Seaman, a tricolour Rough, out of the tricolour Smooth, Ch. Dancerwood Bewitched of Astrellita. He soon gained his Australian title and it was not long before he was in demand at stud. His first mating to Ch. Lioja Plain Copy resulted in Ch. Lioja Mister Dynamic ('Sparky'). In 1989 Jan and Tony exported the first Smooth Collie from Australia into Europe. He was named Lioja Bushtucker Man, and he was sent to Holland to be shown.

SOUTH AFRICA
THE ROUGH COLLIE
The Wiltshire prefix is well-known in South Africa for producing excellent stock. Ch. Wiltshire Conqueror, an outstanding Group winner in 1989, was royally bred from Ch. Wiltshire Hidden Fire out of Ch. Wiltshire Seraphic. His coat was the most beautiful rich sable, and his mane touched the ground. Other Wiltshire winners have won well under English specialist judges, and

Ch. Foxearth Macshands Diamond (Eng. Ch. Astrellita the Silversmith – Eng. Ch. Foxearth Frappant), imported by Denice Tyson.

under well-known all-rounders. Hans and Hella Fricke imported some lovely stock from England – mainly Brylin, Bririch and Tamelia lines. Another well-known prefix is Chellert, owned by Dr Rochelle Ehrlich, who has bred many outstanding Rough Collie Champions.

THE SMOOTH COLLIE

Denice Tyson imported the tricolour Smooth Collie who became Ch. Foxearth Macshands Diamond, sired by Eng. Ch. Astrellita The Silversmith out of Eng. Ch. Foxearth Frappant. She also imported a Smooth bitch – the result of a mating between Ch. Foxearth Winnings the Game at Bothways and Foxearth Flambera – and she became Ch. Foxearth Macshands Ebony. These Collies were the foundation stock for the breed in South Africa. Ch. Foxearth the Tinsmith, who is a full brother to SA Ch. Foxearth Macshands Diamond, has recently sired a litter to Ch. Astrellita Adele in the UK.

SWEDEN
THE ROUGH COLLIE

Think of Sweden, and the name that springs to mind is Steadlyn, now known as Steadwyn. (This is because Mia Ejerstad has married Bernardo Conti and moved to Italy, taking the Steadlyn prefix for herself, and her mother Anja uses the Steadwyn prefix.) Mia and her mother have been showing and breeding since the 1970s, and this partnership has produced some of the finest Rough Collies in the world. They bought a bitch from the Dragonens kennel, owned by Birgitta Holm, to use as a future brood, and almost every Steadlyn and Steadwyn Collie can trace their pedigree back to this bitch. She was Dragonen's Pretty Belinda, sired by Ch. Lynway Shabby Tiger, who was a son of Brettonpark Highlander of Dunsinane. The dam was heavily line-bred to the famous Ch. Ramsey of Rokeby, and from this bloodline the Steadlyn and Steadwyn kennels started to make their mark in the show ring.

In 1979 the first blue merle joined the kennel, with the help of Ulla Eriksson of the Crony kennel: they found a blue dog sired by Int. Ch. Danvis Blue Peter, who was the son of Eng. Aus. Ch. Danvis Ladyvale Blue Mist. He went on to become one of Scandinavia's most successful blue

N. Ch. Cronys Remarkable Silver By Blu: the top winning Rough Collie in Sweden of all time.

dogs, winning the Working Group five times. He also sired Int. N. Dk.It. & It. Club Ch. Steadlyn Zong of Sweden. This bitch had had the most outstanding career, and her name is a legend in Sweden. She was Best in Show seven times, Collie of the Year 1986 and 1988, and she won her Danish title at nine years of age, together with the Reserve World Champion title at the World Show in 1989. She won the same title again at the World Show in 1990, and followed this up by winning her Italian Club Champion title and going on to win the Working Group at the age of ten. This bitch just went from strength to strength. I saw her in Sweden when I co-judged with Mrs Audrey Chatfield in 1987, and she was Best in Show. I last saw her in Italy at home with Mia and Bernardo, aged over twelve, still playing like a youngster and still as beautiful as ever.

In 1983 the partnership bought the young tricolour dog, Lynaire All In Black. He was not too keen on showing, but he was of such quality that he won three CCs and went on to be one of Sweden's most successful tricolour stud dogs of all time. His offspring have won more than one hundred CCs and CACIBs, and he has sired International Champions in all three colours. When he was mated to Zong of Zweden, the result was Int. N. Dk. World Ch. Steadlyn Show Stopper. He has proved to be one of the most consistent winners on the continent, and top winning Rough Collie in Italy in 1990 with many Group wins. He won the World title in 1990 and is the sire of many big winners. Not only has Mia made a name for herself with her Rough Collies, she is also an accomplished artist and she is responsible for the outstanding drawings which illustrate the Breed Standard in this book.

Int. Nor. Danish Ch. Steadlyn Ravishing Saga.   Pro Dog.

Ulla and Eva Eriksson are responsible for some of the finest blue merles. Their Crony Kennel is noted for outstanding colour and superb markings. Ulla Eriksson purchased her first Rough Collie in 1958, later bringing in another two bitches. All three became Champions, two of them becoming International Champions. By using Int. Ch. Sheildon Sterling from Sheil, who lived in Finland, they produced some outstanding Collies, by combining Carramar and Clickham lines and, later on, Danvis breeding. The summer of 1992 saw twelve generations direct from Crony's bitch line.

The kennel made use of the blue merle Int. Ch. Incredibly Blu Di Cambiano while he was staying with them in Sweden, and he produced many Champions – one of them N. Ch. Swedish winner 1990 & 1991 Cronys Remarkable Silver By Blu. He is the top-winning Rough Collie of all time in Sweden with fifteen CCs, twenty CACIBs, two Best in Show at Championship shows, five Best in Show at Collie Club Championship shows, seven Best in Group at Swedish Kennel Club Championship Shows, Collie of the Year in 1989, 1990, and 1991. His half-sister was Collie of the Year in 1987, and winner of eleven CCs.

Ulla and Eva had the honour of being Top Breeders of the Year in the Working Group, and overall twelfth place at the Swedish Kennel Club list of breeders. Twenty-five years ago Ulla Eriksson started the Swedish Collie Club and was secretary for many years; in 1991 she had the honour of being elected to the Disciplinary Committee of the Swedish Kennel Club. She has been judging since 1976 and awards CCs in almost one hundred breeds.

Britt and Inge Slottner of the Marbles Collies are well-known around the shows, and over the years they have bred some beautiful Collies, mainly blue merles and tricolours. The Fairlines kennel, owned by Barbro Bjorkland, is known for both Rough and Smooth Collies. I was very fortunate to visit her home, which is a beautiful old schoolhouse on the edge of a forest. It was such a joy to see all of Barbro's Collies, young and old, Rough and Smooth, all running through the forest in deep snow. I saw Smooth Collies pulling carts of shopping and logs for the fire. The dogs all had lovely warm kennels that were built into the downstairs classroom, and every evening they all came up the winding, wooden staircase to enjoy an evening round the fire with the family.

Ulla Bergh Persson consistently breeds good stock and the Bermarks Rough Collies have been successful in the show ring for Ulla and for others who have bought her dogs. She produces outstanding stock for show and for Obedience. Ulla is also well-known as an international Championship judge.

THE SMOOTH COLLIE

The Swedish Smooth Collie breeders must be congratulated on the development of the breed in their country – some of the finest Smooth Collies in the world are on show at all the major shows in Sweden.

Before coming to England to marry Trevor Hayward, Birgit was well-known for her Glenfields kennel of Rough and Smooth Collies. When Nuch Glenfields Garrison was mated to Astrellita Abba, the result was the outstanding Fairlines Billy the Kid, admired by all who have had the pleasure to judge him. The Fairlines kennel is one of the most prolific breeders of top quality Smooth Collies in Sweden. Billy the Kid sired the beautiful tricolour bitch, Oneways Bloody Mary, a super bitch of sheer quality, with an outstanding head. 'Astrid', as she is known, has done much for the Smooth Collie as a show dog. Astrid's mother was Korad Oneways Ticket, who was sired by the import, Dancerwood Court Jester.

Jester was a full brother to Ch. Dancerwood Bewitched of Astrellita, and he was to sire many top winning Smooth Collies in Sweden. Before he left England, he sired my own Ch. Astrellita the

Fairlines Billy The Kid: The first Smooth Collie to go Best in Show at the Swedish Collie Club Show.

Sw. Ch. Korad One Ways Classic Case (Chess – Oneways Bloody Mary).

Silversmith and Ch. Astrellita the Gunslinger of Newarp. Ch. Astrellita the Silversmith sired Ch. Foxearth the Blacksmith and Ch. Foxearth the Tinsmith, both currently producing top quality Smooth collies – so Jester has left his mark on both sides of the world. Barbro Bjorkland, breeder of the Fairlines Smooth Collies, has had some wonderful results with her breeding programmes, and many top Smooth Collie kennels are grateful to Barbro for her sound knowledge of the breed. Mrs Lyn Westby has judged in Sweden, and her best dog winner was the tricolour dog, Fairlines First Class Lover, and Best of Breed was the litter sister, Fairlines First Class Mistress, a beautiful blue merle that was elegant yet still retained a workmanlike shape.

Jeanette Savlund, who lives in Orebro, must be very proud indeed of her beautiful Smooth Collies. She purchased her first Smooth Collie in 1981, and this was Sw. Fin. Ch. Korad One Way Ticket, sired by Dancerwood Court Jester who was sent out to Sweden from the UK. This bitch, known as Tjorven, was the first Smooth Collie in Sweden to become a full Champion; she also won her title in Finland, and was the first Smooth Collie bitch to pass the temperament test (korning), and so the word Korad prefixes her name. This bitch was also top winning Smooth Collie as she won five CCs, four CACIBs and many Best of Breeds; she was the winner at the Swedish Winners Show in 1986 and 1988.

She was mated in 1984 to Fairlines Billy the Kid, and in the litter was Oneways Tom Collins (one CC), Oneways Ginger Ale (three CCs and one CACIB), and Oneways Bloody Mary, one of my favorite bitches, who won eight CCs, five CACIBs, plus several Best of Breeds and Best in Show awards. She won her Norwegian title at seven years old and was Best of Breed at the Swedish Winners Show in 1987. Ginger Ale was mated back to her father, Billy, in 1986 and produced Sw. Ch. Korad Starlight. She, in turn, was mated to the Rough Collie Bermarks Barley Water, but only one puppy was born. However, Oneways Elvira, as she was called, won seven CCs, one CACIB, six Best of Breed, one Group, and one Best in Show – all this in eight shows. Bloody Mary or Astrid, as she was called, had her first litter in 1987 after being mated to a Rough Collie called Chess, and she produced three Smooths in the litter. They all made their mark: Oneway's Classic Case, a superb coloured blue, went on to win his Korad Sw. Ch. title, along with his sister, Korad Sw. Ch. Oneway's Charming Chenille, and the third littermate won three CCs.

Astrid was so proud of these puppies she mated herself to her half-brother (without telling anyone!) and produced Sw. Ch. N. Ch. Korad Oneways Gunfighter. Astrid's third litter was by Oneways Look Sharp and produced four Smooths – and what a litter this turned out to be! By the age of ten months Oneway's Got to be a Lover had won the title of Eujv 91. He was exported to Finland where he won Europa Winner 91 and Best Opposite Sex under the English judge Trevor Hayward, and by the time he was two years old he had passed his temperament test and become a Champion. His sister SV-91 Oneway's Fatal Charm won eighteen CCs, two CACIBs, sixteen Best of Breeds, two Best in Show and one Group. She also won the title Sw. Winner 91 at fourteen months old, and is the CC record holder in Sweden. Astrid is the only bitch in Sweden that has produced four children who have passed the hard temperament test. Many more beautiful Smooths bred at these kennels have gone on to win top awards in stiff competition. At the biggest show of the year in Sweden at Stockholm in 1991, the Oneways kennel won the award of top breeding kennel, under the English judge John Blake. At this same show all the top winning bitches were from the Oneways kennel.

DENMARK
THE ROUGH COLLIE
Tove and John Holmboe of the Poulsgard kennel applied for their prefix in 1963, and from their first litter came the shaded sable bitch, Poulsgard Dina. This bitch proved to be a super brood bitch and also won a CC. Dina was mated to Int. Dk. Ch. Crony's Golden Duffer and from this litter came their first Champion, Poulsgard's Golden Marki. He was a good show dog, but he was also a defence dog and worked in the Civil Defence force as a rescue dog. In this same litter were the CC winning Poulsgard Golden Lara and Poulsgard Golden Grief. The mating of Dina and Duffer was repeated, and all the kennel's stock goes back to these first Poulsgard dogs.

In 1972 they purchased Antoc Pipes of Pan, bred by Aileen Speding in England, and they also bought the bitch Ravensbeck Carmen Jones. In 1973 they acquired Tavenas Wandering Star and Tavenas Wonder Star, both sired by Geoff Mildon's Ch. Geoffdeon Wayside Boy, and these two dogs were a great asset, both taking their titles. In 1976 Tove and John went to visit Mr and Mrs Eglin of the famous Rokeby kennels in England, and they returned home with a blue bundle of fluff who became Int. Dk. Ch. Europesg Polish Ch. Rokeby Blue by Request. This dog was a son of Knight Porter of Rokeby, and he was the winner of many prizes including a Group. From this

Int. Dk. Ger. VDH Ch. Club Ch. Polish Ch. Johenna Fortune Maker: the top winning Rough Collie in Denmark in 1991 and 1992.

Int. Dk. Ger. VDH Ch. Club Ch. World Winner 1990 Sunsweet Golden Delight and Int. Dk. Ger. VDH Ch. Europesg, Bundessg and World Winner 1985 and 1990 Frazer From Foxearth.

point the kennel went from strength to strength, producing many Champions including Ch. Poulsgard Kalule by Blue, Ch. Poulsgard Midnight Youkay and Int. Ch. Joy Joy Blue, and many more superb Champions. The Poulsgard kennel owned the top winning Rough Collie in Denmark in 1991 and 1992 with Int. Dk. Ger. VDH Ch. Club Ch. Polish Ch. Johenna Fortune Maker. He is one of the few Collies ever to have won a Best in Show at a Danish International show, and was also Best in Show at an International show in Poland.

THE SMOOTH COLLIE

Smooth Collies were introduced to the Poulsgard kennel in 1984 when Sunsweet Golden Delight (Ella) was purchased from Marita Axi in Finland. Ella's wins include Int. Dk. Ger. VDH Ch., Club Ch., World Winner 1990. In 1984 Tove and John acquired Frazer From Foxearth from Trevor and Birgit Hayward in England. He also won Int. Dk. Ger. VDH Ch., Europesg, Bundessg and World Winner in 1985 and 1990. These two outstanding Champions were mated, and they produced four Champions – Ch. Poulsgard's Duvil, Ch. Poulsgard's Dukan, Ch. Poulsgard's Delight and Ch. Poulsgard's Dealer, plus CC-winning Poulsgard's Kunos and Poulsgard's Emma.

Foxearth Forever Loving was imported from Trevor and Birgit to be mated with Frazer, and from this mating came Ch. Poulsgard's Song of Love, Ch. Steela Breeze, Ch. Smooth Passion and Ch. Saltzman. After twenty-nine years of breeding the Poulsgard kennel has an outstanding record of having bred thirty-seven Rough Collie Champions and CC winners, nine Smooth Collie Champions and CC winners, and forty-eight Shetland Sheepdog Champions and CC winners. The policy of this kennel is to know the Standard and to breed to it.

Ch. Vanity Hooligan Duke: Norway's most recent success story.

NORWAY
THE ROUGH COLLIE

The kennels of Dr Per Frey have had Collies for many years. The most recent success is Vanity Hooligan Duke, who won his title at the age of two. Duke also passed the Obedience test and the character test. Also in Norway is the very handsome young blue dog, Hazelside Rough Diamond, sent out by Yvonne Hawthorne from the UK. He is sired by Ingledene Midnight Diamond out of Lowerpark Liberty Belle, who is a daughter of Ch. Lowerpark Star Spangled and Lowerpark Mantilla Lace. Now owned by Mrs Anne Manvik, Rough Diamond is enjoying a super run of wins at the major shows.

FINLAND
THE ROUGH COLLIE

Finland is the home of some outstanding Rough Collie breeders. The Sunsweet kennels, owned by Marita Axi, has consistent winners in all three colours. Many International winners have graced the show ring from these very successful kennels. Marita has been top breeder in Finland for 1982, 1983, 1984, 1985, and 1987, showing the consistency of good breeding. Her dogs are always handled to perfection and shown in beautiful condition. I had the pleasure of judging some of Marita's dogs when I was in Finland in 1990, and all had good length head and sweet expression. I was very impressed with the colour of the blue merles – a really clear blue with excellent markings.

Int. Ch. Sunsweet Up To The Top, owned and bred by Marita Axi in Finland.

Another success story is the Finn Arrow kennels, owned by Mr and Mrs Berggren, and their stock has done much to improve the Rough Collies in Russia. Many top winners in Russia are sired by Finn Arrow dogs. SF Ch. Finn Arrow Bettina has a classic head shape and excellent ear placement. The Berggrens used some of the finest English bloodlines, mainly Rokeby, and the famous Ladypark lines, and have gone on to produce some really outstanding Rough Collies that could win anywhere in the world. The latest Champion from the Finn Arrow kennels is Finn Arrow Black Yarmouth, who has three CCs and two CACIBs, and looks set to continue keeping this prefix to the fore. The Snowpaw kennels, owned by Tuija Heikkila, is also well-known for its excellent Rough Collies.

THE SMOOTH COLLIE

Irja Rekola started her Karenclans kennel of Smooth Collies with a brood bitch of outstanding quality – Int. North Ch. NW 83 Dalimattas Kortis Karamell, who was best Smooth Collie for the years 1983, 1984, 1985, 1986 and 1987. She was not only a highly successful show dog, but had also done very well at Working Trials, and was an official Civil Defence dog, used for rescuing people lost in forests or in natural disasters.

Irja kept three puppies from the first litter, sired by Dancerwood Court Jester, and these puppies were to begin a Smooth Collie breeding programme. From this litter came the well-known Karenclans Court Lover, who was an excellent stud dog, siring some outstanding Smooth Collies – he was the best sire in 1988. After taking back some of Court Lover's daughters and using different stud dogs to swell the gene pool, Irja decided to import Foxearth Frankie, who was sired by the famous Ch. Sylbecq Draught Guinness at Foxearth, out of Ch. Foxearth Frappant. Frankie was soon to become one of Finland's top stud dogs.

Int. Dk. Dalimattas Kortis Karamell: Best Smooth Collie in Finland 1983, 1984, 1985, 1986 and 1987.

Irja's latest import, Ch. Foxearth Freeman, seems to suit all the bitches sired by Frankie. In fact, one of Freeman's puppies was Best Puppy in Show at the big national show in Lhati, Finland. I judged the bitch named Baubons Classy Cocktail Mystery, and sent her through to win the title under another English judge. Foxearth Freeman's progeny are now ready to start Working Trials, and one has started his Civil Defence training, showing that not only are the Karenclans Smooth Collies beautiful, they are also clever, proving that Irja Rekola has gone from strength to strength, breeding outstanding and intelligent Smooth Collies.

Seija Lehmusto of the Cepu Jesse kennels confines her breeding to Smooth Collies, and she has enjoyed considerable success at the shows she has attended. At the International Lhati show, I awarded the Reserve CC to Sepu Jess. This handsome, sable dog has won twenty-two honour prizes, sixteen Certificates and nine Best of Breed awards. Helvi, Minna and Piia Manninen of the Kangasvukon kennels, are the proud owners of a beautiful, young Smooth tricolour bitch, named Karenclans Rosy Anemone. She was sired by Eng. Ch. Foxearth Freeman and was out of Karenclans Gardenia. She is the first Smooth Collie for this kennel, and they hope to make a name for themselves breeding good Smooth Collies. 'Gitte', as she is called, has done some very useful winning. She was Best Bitch Puppy at Turku in 1991, and I awarded her Best Junior Bitch at the Lhati show. This young bitch will be the foundation for this kennel, showing how important it is to start breeding with good stock. She has a good front, excellent quarters, good, strong feet, and a happy nature – all essential ingredients to pass on to future generations.

The Sunsweet kennels, owned by Marita Axi, breeds Smooth Collies, as well as her hugely successful Rough Collies. Dalimatass Future Flora is a beautiful sable bitch, with all the qualities I like to see in a Smooth Collie bitch. She has a correct neck and good front, the correct length of back and sound hindquarters. Her ears are perfectly set and are constantly alert, and she has a beautiful expressive eye. She has a harsh well-fitting jacket of the correct texture. I admired this bitch so much that I would have imported her, given the chance. Her tally of wins from March 1990 to April 1991 included twelve Best of Breeds, twelve CCs and four CACIBs – an outstanding career.

The Snowpaw kennels, owned by Tuija Heikkila, is best known for its excellent Rough Collies. However, the Smooth Collie is not neglected, and the young tricolour male, Dalimattas Future Flipper has enjoyed considerable success in the show ring. Tuija hopes to combine beautiful Smooth Collies with good working lines – and with a male of this quality, the Smooth Collie's future in Finland appears to be assured.

RUSSIA
THE ROUGH COLLIE
The Russian Collie breeders are to be congratulated for their perseverance – it must be a nightmare trying to breed and rear good stock in a country where there are so many shortages. The vast majority of the Rough Collies in Russia are bred from stock imported from Finland, and, as many

Winnie Gett sired by Finn Arrow Black Jockey (Finland) out of Winnie Ze Zlate Jalny (Russia), bred by S. Kazova in Moscow.

of the top breeders in Finland import from England, most of the pedigrees contain top English bloodlines in the third and fourth generations.

Mrs Audrey Chatfield made history when she was invited to judge a Collie Club show in the Soviet Union, as it was then called. The show was held in Estonia in 1989, and over 250 Rough Collies came to be judged by the first English judge to officiate. What a mammoth task it must have been to judge so many Collies! In Mrs Chatfield's write-up of the show she stated that many of the Collies lacked substance, and I am sure this must be due to the lack of the high-quality dog food that is readily available to us. Among the Rough Collies shown under Mrs Chatfield was a blue bitch shown in the veteran class. Her name was Barnehof's Ocelot Girl, aged ten years, and she went on to be Best Bitch in Show. She was sired by English import Bririch Blue Ocean and imported from Sweden. Best in Show on that day was the sable dog, Finn Arrow Golden Duffy, owned by Ege Maas, imported from Finland and sired by Antoc Lord of the Dance.

Most of the photographs I have seen of Rough Collies in Russia are Collies sired by the Finnish import Finn Arrow Black Jockey. With the restrictions on visas and currency now being lifted, the Russian breeders are striving to improve the Rough Collie by importing new stud dogs and brood bitches.

At the present time there are no Smooth Collies in Russia.

HUNGARY
THE ROUGH COLLIE
Mr Peter Harsa'nyi is the President of the Hungarian British Shepherd Dogs Club. The club was founded in 1958 and has 485 members; sixty-two per cent are Rough Collie breeders, twenty-five per cent are Old English Sheepdog breeders, ten per cent are Bearded Collie breeders and three per cent breed Shetland Sheepdogs. There are no breeders of Border Collies or Smooth Collies now living in Hungary. In 1991 417 Rough Collie litters were born, with a total of 2,260 puppies.

The most successful Rough Collie dog in 1990 was the import Sandiacre Streets Ahead. This dog was bred by Mrs S. Wigglesworth and owned by Janos Balazsovits, and was Hungarian

Hungarian Ch. Sandiacre Streets Ahead: the top winning Rough Collie in Hungary.

Champion 1990/91. The most successful bitch in 1991 was the lovely-coloured Koakoi Ulla, bred by Peter Harsa'nyi. I gave this bitch the CACIB in Vienna in 1991. She has won many other awards including three CACIBs, five CACs, Junior Winner, and Best in Show. The top Rough dog in 1991 was the brother of Ulla, a heavy-coated tricolour with excellent body shape, and good head and eye. He was Junior Hungarian Champion, 1990 Veronz Junior Europe Winner, Junior Club Winner, the winner of two Reserve CACs, two Reserve CACIBs, five CACs, two CACIBs, Group winner, and Best in Show – a very impressive show year. Another well-known import is Sandiacre Split Decision, bred by Mrs Wigglesworth and owned by Janos Balazsovits.

Hungary has a strong band of Rough Collie breeders all striving to produce sound, well constructed Rough Collies. There are only a couple of Smooths shown in this country, and they are both Rough-bred. When I judged in Budapest I was pleased to see the quality of many of the exhibits, and they were all well groomed and well presented in the ring.

GERMANY
THE ROUGH COLLIE

An import to really hit the top spots was Lynway Seldom Sober, purchased by Birgit and Peter Fricke, who live in Germany. This dog was sent out by the Clark family in Nottingham, UK, and in his new home this dog won the titles International Ch., German Ch., VDH Ch., Bundessieger 1990 (one of the highest awards on offer), was top winning dog 1990, and was Reserve World Champion 1991. Seldom Sober now has winning offspring in many European countries. Another top kennel is that of Hans Jurgen and Jutta Bicher, who have been breeding good stock since 1973. They own the imported sable dog, Corydon Tiger Topps, who is the winner of Austrian Jugendbundessieger 1989 and Junior Winner 1989 and Austrian Junior Champion 89. He went on to be Belgian winner 1991 and took the CACIB in Vienna, winning in Germany, Czechoslovakia and many other countries.

A kennel always to the fore in Germany is that of Margrit and Gunter Rall. I have judged their dogs on a few occasions, and I have also judged alongside Gunter Rall, who is well respected for his opinion on the Rough Collie. The Ralls have bred many Champions. Among their latest successes is German Youth Ch. and European Youth Ch. VDH Ch. Golden Rocco Vom Bienenfleiss, who gained his German title in 1990. The Vom Hause Reinhard Collies are known in many countries, and many top winning Collies are bred from Vom Hause Reinhard stock. The 1991 World Champion Jet Black Vom Hause Reinhard has had a superb show career, winning many titles. Her grandfather was World Champion 85 VDH Dt. Ch. Cookie Vom Hause Reinhard, and her dam was World Champion 86.

THE SMOOTH COLLIE

After the war the Smooth Collie was extinct in Germany, and it was not until 1961 that Mrs Inge Harth imported a tricolour Smooth bitch from Mrs Chatfield of the Dunsinane Rough Collies. This was Donna Anona of Dunsinane, a daughter of the famous Rough dog, Westcarrs Blue Minoru out of the Smooth bitch Peterblue Donna Rosa. She arrived in whelp to the blue merle Ch. Hughley Hush Puppy Blue. In the meantime the blue merle dog Selskars Thane was imported from England to Holland. Donna Anona was mated to him, and from this litter a bitch was retained for breeding. She was mated to her uncle, Don Argos of Dunsinane, and produced the Smooth tricolour, Int. Ch. Nonie Vom Ihlpol.

Another well-known breeder of Rough Collies, Dr Hofmann, imported a tricolour Smooth bitch, Peterblue Miranda, who very quickly gained her title. She was mated to the blue merle Rough Collie, Ch. Dunsinane Blue Arrow of Leawyn, and one of the resulting puppies became an International Champion.

Guenther Schoebel first fell in love with the Smooth Collie in 1959, but at that time was unable to have one. He eventually acquired two sable Smooth Collies – Northing and Norma II Vom Hamburger Wappen, who both became International Champions. To this day Mr Schoebel retains his interest in the Smooth Collie, and I was fortunate to meet him when he came to my kennels to collect his new Smooth Collie stud dog, Astrellita Anonymous, a tricolour from Ch. Astrellita Adele.

BELGIUM
THE ROUGH COLLIE
The Beinn Mhor Collies of Jean Pierre and Patricia Daenen have done some useful breeding of Rough Collies, and Of The Colliery is another well-known kennel producing some really good Collies. Karel and Christiane Gelissen of Genk in Belgium imported the handsome blue merle, Pelido Licence to Thrill, and they also own the lovely tricolour bitch, Brylin Dark Delight, who is keeping the kennel name to the fore. Annick Antoine is the proud owner of the De Gold Collies in Belgium. She owns the blue merle, Ch. Rock and Blues Di Cambiano, and imported Pelido Kings Council. Kings Council sired the truly handsome Love Story of Trefoli Farm, owned by Nadia Vanneste. Mario and Colette Castronovo have some excellent Rough Collies in all three colours. I came across one of their lovely puppies when I was judging in Switzerland, and again when I was judging in Luxemburg.

THE SMOOTH COLLIE
There are only two Smooth Collies currently living in Belgium. Astrellita Black Alf is a tricolour male, sired by Crossfell Precious Jet out of Astrellita Alicia, who is sister to my own Ch. Astrellita Adele. So far, Alf has won seven CACs and his Belgian title. The other Smooth is Beony Chelsea from Astrellita; she is still a youngster and has been sent out as a future mate for Alf. Chelsea is a daughter of Astrellita Singing the Blues and Newarp Cat Dancer. Singing the Blues is a daughter of Ch. Adele, so there will be some good line breeding behind the Smooth Collies in Belgium.

HOLLAND
THE ROUGH COLLIE
The Neo Konia kennels are breeders of blue merles and tricolours in Holland, and some very lovely dogs have been bred over the last twenty years,

Astrellita Angel Tears (Ch. Ladyfayre Blue Lagoon at Karava – Ch. Astrellita Adele), owned by Debbie Palmer in Paris.

THE SMOOTH COLLIE
The kennels of Marijke Spiering and Marijke Van Der Noordaa Meertens have been breeding Smooth Collies for a great number of years, and their Smooth Collies are known all over the Continent. They have imported stock from Kay Alexander and Birgit and Trevor Hayward, and they have produced top winners, including Farthings Made of Stardust, who is a Dutch, Belgian, Int. Ch., Lux. Ch., World Ch. 1990, winning fourteen CAC and CACIBs. He is the Best Home-bred Collie 1989 and 1990 of the Dutch Collie Club, and Best Smooth Collie of the Dutch Collie Club 1990. He is the first Smooth Collie in the twenty-five year history of the Dutch Collie Club's Championship show to go Best in Show, which he did in 1991. 'Joey', as he is known, is a grandson of Ch. Sylbecq Draught Guinness at Foxearth.

SWITZERLAND
THE SMOOTH COLLIE

It is only in the last few years that Smooth Collies have been shown at all the major shows. In 1980 I met a young man at Crufts who was interested in obtaining a Smooth Collie to work cattle in the high meadows of Switzerland. He wanted a strong-boned dog of good character, who would also be obedient. He wanted the dog to be a blue merle, to be show quality, and, if at all possible, to look the same as Ch. Astrellita the Silversmith. A tall order – but I accepted the challenge and said I would reserve him a dog from our next litter, who I hoped would meet all these requirements.

My very beautiful Ch. Dancerwood Bewitched of Astrellita was mated to Ch. Cathenbrae Polar Moon at Pelido, a Rough Collie of the most superb colour, a dog of substance and good character. I was very lucky with this litter and kept back a handsome blue merle dog to be collected by

Ch. Gerrilee Blue Alf and his dam Int. Ch. Astrellita Blue Serena, in Switzerland.

Gerald Martin and his partner, Willie Chappuis. This dog grew into a true Collie, working the cattle during the week, and being shown fearlessly at all the Championship shows in Europe to gain the title of Int. Ch. Astrellita Blue Macho. From this same litter came the equally famous blue merle bitch Ch. Astrellita Blue Movie at Glenmist.

Macho worked so well and won so many admirers that Gerald and Willie decided to buy another Smooth from my kennel. When he heard that my Ch. Astrellita Adele had been mated to Ch. Astrellita the Silversmith, he promptly booked two puppies. The dog, Astrellita the Accomplice, was for work and show; and the pretty blue bitch, Astrellita Blue Serena, was for showing and breeding. In October 1990 the first litter of Smooth Collies for twenty-six years was born in Switzerland. Serena whelped seven puppies to the tricolour dog Opilio Sound of Kilbrannan, bred by Mrs Edvige Ubiali.

I have visited Gerald and Willie many times in Switzerland and I always go to see Macho work the cattle. To see a dog you have bred do the work it was originally bred for, is a very rewarding feeling. I last saw Macho in June 1991, when he was ten years of age, and he was still busy working, while his sister, Blue Movie, had just won Reserve Top Smooth Collie Of The Year, after going Best of Breed at Crufts earlier in the year.

ITALY
THE ROUGH COLLIE

The influence of top-winning English imports can be seen in many of the Rough Collie kennels in Italy. This includes the kennels of Luciano Bernini, who has also bred many Champions bearing his Del Narciso prefix. One of his most consistent winners in 1990 was It. Ch. Social Ch. Abbey Del Narciso, owned by Alan Jones, who left England some years ago to help Luciano with his

A group of Steadlyn blue merles; (left to right) Int. N. Dk. It. It. Club Ch. Steadlyn Zong of Zweden, Steadlyn Snowdance (eight months), Steadlyn Snow Goddess (standing), Steadlyn Fairy Snow, Steadlyn Snow Rose (eight months), Shep's Huckleberry Boy (three months).

huge kennel of Collies. Alan also owned It. Ch. Teresa Del Narciso and It. Ch. Nina Del Narciso. I awarded Alan's Rough Collie, Ch. Glenalan Troopers Boy at Loriant his Social title.

Franco Caselli (Figli Del Vento) is another important breeder of Rough Collies. He is a fan of Lisa and Peter Burtenshaw's Pelido kennels and has imported many dogs from this source. Franco has an impressive stud team, all with superb breeding. Among them is the imported Ch. Myberns Mandrian, Ch. Pelido Midnight Scandal, Ch. Pelido Foreigner, and the lovely sable dog, Int. Ch. Langili Say No More.

Maria Teresa Garabelli has bred many fine Champions and she was responsible for sending her beautiful blue merle dog, Int. Ch. Incredibly Blue di Cambiano to England. He was used on many English bitches, and now his lovely colour is incorporated in English bloodlines. The Cambiano kennels have made an impact on the Rough Collie scene in Italy with dogs such as It. Ch. Collie Club Ch. Top Tricolour de Cambiano and VDH Europa Ch. Lord Blue Night.

The Steadlyn Collies, owned by Mia Ejerstad Conti who has made her home in Italy with her husband, Bernardo, are also highly influential in the breed. They form one of Italy's top kennels.

THE SMOOTH COLLIE
The kennel of Edvige Ubiali of the Opilio kennels has imported many English Smooth Collies and has bred some outstanding Smooths. Dogs from these kennels have won major awards all over the continent. Their stud dogs are widely used and produce excellent stock.

IRELAND
THE ROUGH COLLIE

The early history of Rough Collies in Ireland goes back to the 1880s, when the sport of showing dogs became popular. In 1892 the Irish Collie Club was formed, and this club still exists today, based in Northern Ireland under English Kennel Club rules. The foundation meeting and all subsequent meetings up until 1908 were held in Dublin, although members was drawn from all parts of Ireland. The club was run by a committee consisting of some seven members, and from a perusal of the minutes it would appear to have been a somewhat autonomous body, guaranteeing classes, allocating specials and prizes, and nominating judges at all shows where the breed was scheduled throughout Ireland.

Ir. Ch. Peblu Golden Strand, owned and bred by Grenville Francis, Co. Down.

It is not generally known that the present club is an amalgamation of two clubs, viz the Irish Collie Club founded in 1892 and the North of Ireland Collie Club founded in 1904. Both these clubs were very active in all aspects of the breed, and a number of officers and members were common to both. At a meeting held in Dundalk on September 8th 1908 preliminary steps were taken for the amalgamation of the two clubs. This was ratified at a joint meeting of the members of the two clubs in Belfast. In 1922 the Irish Kennel Club was formed, and Rough Collie registrations in that year were twenty-two; for the following two years they stood at twenty-three; they dipped to fifteen in 1925, but more than doubled to thirty-three the following year.

The present Irish Collie Club, with the exception of the Scottish Collie Club, is the oldest of the breed clubs in the British Isles and is probably among the oldest breed clubs in the world. The present membership of the club is around 150, and it is a strong club, promoting the breed wherever possible, both at home and overseas. Three shows are organised each year: the Annual Open Breed Show, the Open All Breed Show, and the Championship Show, all of which are well attended. In fact, the club was only granted Championship status in 1988, and this was after some twenty years of appeals.

The very first Rough Champion under Irish KC rules was Mr Allen's Arvon Positive, a tricolour dog. In 1926 the All Ireland Collie Club was founded by Mr P. Sinnott, who became the Secretary. Mr Sinnott made up six Irish Champions – the last one in 1968. He also ran his Rough Collies in Field Trials with sheep.

During the early seventies Mr and Mrs J. Kirk of the Cregagh prefix emerged as a force to be reckoned with. Their lines are based on a mixture of Rokeby and Sandiacre, and this kennel still continues breeding to this day. A major development in the breed in Ireland was the first breed Championship Show, which was held in 1977. The judge elect for this show was Lyn Westby of the Lowerpark Collies. From this point, the Rough went from strength to strength, with the formation of the Rough Collie Club of Ireland in 1979. The Collies now had two Championship shows and three Open shows per year. Enthusiasm for the breed came to a peak in 1970, with entries at the Irish Championship Show on St Patrick's Day reaching 127 dogs. Entries were 123 dogs in 1985, and 114 in 1986.

During this time a number of new breeders emerged, but Mr and Mrs Kirk continued to fly the flag with Ch. Rokeby Rorty of Cregagh and his very famous son, Int. Ch. Cregagh Henry Higgins. Henry was a beautiful sable, and was six times Best in Show (all Breeds), including St Patrick's Day IKC Show. The Joshren kennels, owned by Mr and Mrs Walsh, also came to the forefront. This kennel was founded in the early seventies, basing their lines on Corydon and Bririch breeding. During the last decade they have bred nine

Ir. Ch. Lasheen Simply Red of Lynway: top Rough Collie in Eire, 1991.   E. J. F. Steele.

Champions, the most well-known being Ch. Corydon C'est Magnifique. The Snugborough prefix, owned by Mr and Mrs Finnan, has also made an impact with Ir. Eng. Ch. Akdeniz Peter Piper.

The first Southern Irish Rough Collie Champion was Ir. Ch. Junior Ralveras, owned by John Walsh. This dog was born in 1975, sired by Cathenbrae Gay Cavalier out of Meelick Lass. John Walsh has campaigned many Collies to their titles in Southern Ireland, such as Ir. Ch. Joshren Gallant Cavalier (Ir. Ch. Corydon C'est Magnifique – Corydon Aunt Abigayle at Joshren), and the top Rough Collie in Eire 1991, Ir. Ch. Lasheen Simply Red of Lynway (Ch. Lynway Sandnocker – Marridion Merry Maiden of Lasheen). In fact, Red is the only Collie ever to have won a Working Group, and this achievement can never be equalled, as in Eire the Group has now been divided and Collies are in the Pastoral Group. Red has subsequently gone on to win the Pastoral Group.

To become an Irish Champion, a dog must obtain 40 Green Star points. A Green Star has a value of between 1 to 10 points, and this number is determined by the number of dogs exhibited on the day. The 40 points must be obtained as follows:
A. Four wins of 5 points or more under four different judges.
B. Two wins of 5 points or more plus one win of 10 points under 3 different judges.
C. Three wins of 5 points or more plus a group win under 4 different judges.

A dog will not be entitled to be registered as a Champion unless one of the above combinations is included in the 40 points, so it is far from easy for a dog to gain its title. In fact, even with a very good dog, this can take at least two years. In Ireland it is also possible to win the title of Annual Champion, which is won by the dog who wins the most Green Star points in excess of 30 points in any calendar year. Between 1926 and 1976 there were 29 dogs who gained the title of Irish Champion.

There are at present no Smooth Collies being bred or shown in Ireland.

Chapter Fourteen

THE STUD DOG

From the early days, many stud dogs, Rough and Smooth have played a part in bringing about the Collie that we know today. However, the stud dog has been prey to the whims of fashion, and one dog may become extremely popular and be used by nearly all available bitches. This trend started right at the beginning of the Collie's breed history when the Rough Collie Trefoil, born in 1873, was the dog of the moment. Unfortunately, this can lead to future problems which may have an adverse effect on the breed. As far as Rough Collies are concerned, this has never been a problem because of the vast number of Rough Collie sires available. This gives a variety of type, and the owner of a good bitch always has a wide range of dogs to choose from. This is not true of the Smooth Collie, where the gene pool is very small, and certain dogs have become fashionable and have attracted far too many bitches. The Smooth Collie is now very closely line-bred, and the situation is exacerbated with the English Kennel Club's refusal to register the offspring of Rough/Smooth matings. I fear that we will have to turn to the Kennel Club for special permission to use Rough Collies again in the not too distant future, or we will have to rely on imports from overseas to enhance the Smooth Collie gene pool.

KEEPING A STUD DOG
Many small kennels never keep stud dogs, and this applies to many breeds. So unless your dog is a consistent winner or known to be a good producer it is just not worth having another mouth to feed. After all, a stud dog cannot mate a bitch every week of his life. The same criteria apply to both Rough and Smooth Collies, and the only stud dog worth keeping is a top quality Champion that produces sound and winning stock to different lines of bitches.

Having taken this point to heart, let us assume that you have bought or even bred your own stud dog. It is likely that this dog will be used for breeding to your own bitches and will also be offered at public stud in the hope that you will earn some stud fees. The next step is to decide at what age your Collie should start his stud career. If the dog is very keen and is willing and able to mate a bitch even at the early age of ten months, then let him do so. This will not harm him in any way, providing the mating is fully supervised. The dog at this stage must be handled very carefully, and, at all costs, the dog must never be left alone with a bitch in season – she could well attack him and put him off forever.

THE MATING
When you are preparing your Collie for his first mating, it is important to ensure that he does not have a full stomach, and to plan the day so he is well-rested before the bitch is due to arrive. It is a

good idea to use an experienced bitch when you have a maiden dog; she will know what to expect and will not be so inclined to snap at him. No two dogs behave in the same way when it comes to mating. Some dogs mature quicker than others, showing a great interest from an early age. The signs to watch for are the dog that cocks its leg at an early age, and eagerly sniffs his kennel mates. However, some dogs never take any such interest, and this type will never make a good stud dog. You cannot offer a dog at stud if he will not perform when asked. Many bitches travel great distances to be mated, and time is a great factor to be taken into consideration as most bitches will only stand for a few days, and word soon gets around that the dog is reluctant to perform. Most dogs will eventually mate a bitch; a keen youngster will mate with no trouble at all. However, some dogs refuse bitch after bitch with no apparent reason.

As stated, it is always best to use an experienced bitch, who has had a few litters, to start your dog off on his stud career, but if a brood bitch is not available, try your dog with one of his kennel mates that he is familiar with. Unless you have a real Romeo, always insist that the bitch visits the dog. He will perform much better on home ground; if he is away from home he will be too busy sniffing new territory. If possible, always try to use the same area each time so the dog knows that he is going to have a bitch. Make sure it is a quiet spot away from any other dogs and other household noises. The stud dog should be allowed to run about for a while and lift his leg if he so wishes; this is most natural when courting and he should not be scolded for doing so. If the bitch is willing, let them play for a short while, but keep a sharp eye on the bitch in case she should growl and put the dog off.

If all seems well, allow the dog to mount the bitch. Here the Smooth Collie has an advantage over the long-coated Collie as most bitches have lovely long petticoats, and they often get in the way during a mating. In fact, I always tie back the petticoats with some bandage, making sure that no fine hairs are lying across the vulva, as this can be painful to the dog when he tries to mount the bitch. It helps if you spread some vaseline around the edge of the vulva, leaving the way clear for a trouble-free mating. As the dog mounts the bitch, it advisable to have someone to hold the bitch on a collar in order to keep her standing steady to receive the dog. If the bitch is a maiden bitch, it can make matters a little easier if you apply a little vaseline on the tip of the finger, and insert it just inside the vaginal passage.

It is extremely important that you do not allow the young stud dog to fool around at this stage; he must always come round to where you want him. Mating is made much easier if you assist by helping the dog to penetrate by holding the bitch underneath, and then placing the left hand flat under the bitch, from the side between her hindlegs, and placing the first and second fingers either side of the vulva. In this manner, the exact position of the penis can be felt, and no mistakes are made. Once the dog has made contact and penetrated, make sure the bitch is held firmly, as at this stage she may get jumpy and try to pull away. Talk to the bitch calmly, and restrain her if she tries to struggle.

When the dog has tied inside her, he may remain over the bitch turned to one side, or turned back to back. If the bitch cries out, it is important to reassure the dog that he has done nothing wrong. For novice owners the word 'tie' needs explanation. Most mammals are equipped with Cowper's glands which eject semen swiftly. The dog does not have these glands and can only emit semen drip by drip. As the penis enters the vagina it begins to swell gradually until, at about the middle of the penis there is a very pronounced bulbous swelling which makes it impossible for the dog to retract. At the time that the penis is swelling, the muscles of the bitch contract round this swelling and may hold tightly for a few seconds or as long as an hour or more – I supervised a tie that lasted an hour and ten minutes! However, the norm for a tie is around ten to fifteen minutes, but do be prepared for longer. When the dogs are standing comfortably, you can relax your hold a little, and take hold of the dog and bitch's tails and give your back a rest. The pair will come apart when they are ready, and not before. A successful mating may take place without a tie, and large litters of puppies have been born following a mating of this kind. If the bitch is a maiden, it may be a good idea to offer two matings, leaving a day between the matings, if possible.

BREEDING CONTRACTS
Before any mating takes place, you should have a written agreement regarding stud fees. It should be made quite clear that the fee is for the service, not for the results. Like many breeders, I always offer a free service if a bitch misses, but this is not obligatory. Sometimes the bitch's owner will ask you to take a puppy instead of a stud fee. This may not always be convenient, but if the bitch is known for producing good stock, it could be to your advantage.

If you have a good stud dog who is winning well in the show ring, it is wise to have a stud card printed. This can be illustrated with a photo, showing the dog to his best advantage, and it should include the dog's pedigree, a statement that the dog has been found clear of Progressive Retinal Atrophy (PRA) and Collie Eye Anomaly (CEA), and state that the dog has a good hip score. Keep your stud dog clean and well-groomed: you never know when he may have a visit, and he should always look in top condition. Feed good nourishing food, keep your dog wormed, and ensure his vaccinations are up to date.

INFLUENTIAL STUD DOGS
In the early days of the breed the Rough Collie Ch. Metchley Wonder was winning well and during the early 1800s he was used extensively at stud. He sired Ch. Christopher who was sold to America for the fantastic sum of £1000 – an amazing sum at the time. Later Ch. Parbold Piccolo made a significant contribution siring six Champions, including Ch. Anfie Model. Piccolo was exported to America in the early 1900s, and his son Model was used to such an extent that much in-breeding showed up in pedigrees on both sides of the Atlantic. 1912 saw the first of many Laund Champions, bred by Mr W. Stansfield, and their influence was far-reaching. The Eden prefix came on the scene at this time, and along with the Laund and Backwood kennels many beautiful Rough Collies made their way into the history of the breed. Ch. Magnet, born in 1921, proved to be a prepotent sire, who before going to the United States sired many outstanding Champions. This dog had many virtues and was very dominant for type, passing on good head qualities.

During the Second World War many kennels were reduced to keeping very few dogs; it was a very difficult time for dogs and owners alike. Mrs George of the Beulahs kennels kept her kennels going and produced the first post-war Champion, Ch. Beulahs Golden Futureson. He, in turn, sired Beulahs Golden Flora who, when mated to Eden Examine, produced four puppies. One of these puppies was the famous Ch. Lad of Ladypark. He sired many Champions including the handsome Ch. Ugony's Golden Son O Lad of Rifflesea, bred by Miss D. M. Young. In fact, Miss Young became one of the true stalwarts of the breed, and in 1991 she judged Smooth Collies at Crufts.

In 1947 Int. Ch. Lochinvar of Ladypark, the most famous of all post-war sires, was born. He was a dominant sable and consistently passed on his superb style and lovely temperament to bitches of different type. From this stock came the many Ladypark Champions and the well-known Pattingham kennels owned by Mrs M. Franklin. She went on to breed the outstanding dog, Ch. Pattingham Pacemaker, who was one of my particular favourites. He had a beautiful head, a lovely eye, and such style; he gained many admirers when he won the Working Group at Crufts in 1964.

Ch. Lowerpark Moonlighter at Corydon, proving to be a dominant sire, pictured with three of his children (left to right): Corydon Moon Goddess, Corydon Moon Miracle and Corydon Silver Moon.

Sandiacre Softly Softly: sire of five English Champions and numerous Champions worldwide.

Pelido Black Prince: a sire of Champions in all three colours.

It was after seeing this dog that I fell in love with the Rough Collie. The Antoc kennels, owned by Aileen Speding, were well to the fore at this time, and many of her beautiful dogs graced the show ring. Around this time many new kennels started, such as Duntiblae, Bririch, Jesfire and Dunsinane, and the Rough Collie became increasingly popular. The dog of this era must surely be Dazzler of Dunsinane, bred by Audrey Chatfield, an International judge, who has done so much for the Collie fraternity all over the world in forming the International Collie Society. Dazzler was to change the whole Collie scene by stamping his exquisite expression on his progeny. His sweet expressive eye placement was so dominant that you could spot any Dazzler offspring at a glance. In his first litter to Witchcraft of Rokeby (who later became a Champion), he sired Ch. Royal Ace of Rokeby and the lovely Ch. Romney of Rokeby, who had the longest petticoats I have ever seen. Ace went on to sire twelve Champions, and I used the handsome Ch. Ramsey of Rokeby on my bitch, Deloraine Dilemma. From the litter I kept Astrellita Alona, a truly beautiful bitch, and she produced Astrellita Able Seaman. He, in turn, sired two English Smooth Champions, bringing his wonderful expression into the Smooth lines.

One of the few tricolours that Ch. Ramsey of Rokeby sired was Mr and Mrs Blake's Ch. and Aust. Ch. Corydon Quinault, who was successful in the show ring. Mr and Mrs Blake bred and owned some outstanding Rough Collies, and many became famous worldwide. One of the best, in my opinion, was the shaded sable dog Ch. Little Caesar at Corydon, who was full brother to Ch. Dameral Aristides, bred by Mr and Mrs Field. It was a sad day for Britain when Caesar left this country for Australia – their gain was Britain's loss. I think that Caesar could have gone down in breed history as one of the outstanding Rough Collie sires.

Ch. Arranbrook Mr Chips of Aberhill was a popular dog in the 1980s, and he sired a total of eleven Champions. Mr G. Mildon's Ch. Geoffdon Lawmaker was another successful stud dog, and he sired the outstanding tricolour dog, Ch. Karava Kornishman. The Sandiacre kennels produced some first-class Collies at this time, although I have never seen a Sandiacre tricolour in the ring. Sandiacre Softly Softly sired five Champions, and Brettonpark Highlander of Dunsinane sired eight Champions. At this time the Pelido kennels, owned by of Peter and Lisa Burtenshaw, bred

Ch. Sybecq Draught Guinness at Foxearth: a superb Champion in his own right, and to date he has sired ten Champions. *Dalton.*

Pelido Black Prince, a big tricolour dog full of quality, and he made a name for himself by siring Champions in all three colours. One of the most famous of these was Ch. Cathenbrae Polar Moon at Pelido, and when I saw this handsome blue merle dog I just had to use him on my Champion Smooth collie bitch, Ch. Dancerwood Bewitched at Astrellita, thus incorporating all these beautiful Rough Collie lines to enhance the Smooth Collies of the future.

The early Smooth Collies were bred from Rough/Smooth matings. Mr F. Wildgoose (Canute) did a lot for the early Smooths; one of his first dogs was Canute Fascination, bred by Mr Smalley in 1901. In 1902 a litter was bred that produced the Smooth Ch. Canute Perfection who, in turn, sired Ch. Canute Model. Some excellent Smooth Collies came down from this stock, and one Champion, Ch. Quality of Dunkirk, sired by Fascination, was the dam of Ch. Eastwood Eminent. Another outstanding Smooth Collie that was the result of a Rough/Smooth mating was Ch. Eastwood Extra, winner of twenty-seven CCs.

Among the most prolific Smooth stud dogs in the 1970s were the outstanding Ch. Chicnoir Midnight Sultan, a tricolour that has passed on his many qualities, and the sable Hughley Honey Dew. Sultan, when mated to Astrellita Love Affair, produced Ch. Foxearth Goldfever, who was a beautiful rich sable dog. Astrellita Love Affair also inherited this lovely colour. Sultan also produced the blue merle Champions, Ch. Glenmist Blue Lodestone and Ch. Glenmist Rough Diamond. Their dam was the lovely Ch. Astrellita Blue Movie at Glenmist. Ch. Astrellita the Silversmith sired Ch. Foxearth the Tinsmith and Ch. Foxearth the Blacksmith. Ch. Foxearth Goldfever sired the most prolific stud dog of all time, Ch. Draught Guinness at Foxearth, who has been top sire for the last few years, siring many Champions and top winning Smooth Collies.

Ch. Astrellita the Gunslinger sired Ch. Newarp Silver Moonlight, who, when mated to Draught Guinness, produced two top winning Smooth Collies – Ch. Newarp Silver Moonbeam and her brother Ch. Newarp Silver Scimitar. The biggest mistake I ever made was when I let Dancerwood Court Jester leave my kennels to go to Sweden. However, although I regretted the loss, Jester certainly made a name for himself in his new home. He has sired some outstanding Smooth Collies in Scandinavia, and his progeny are to be seen winning top spots in Sweden and Finland. Many of these notable Smooth Collie sires have Rough Collie bloodlines dominantly in their pedigrees, proving yet again how essential it is to have mixed lines.

Chapter Fifteen

THE BROOD BITCH

If you have shown your Rough or Smooth Collie bitch with some success, it is very likely that you will want to breed from her. The choice of stud dog must be of the utmost importance, as choosing the wrong mate will not only be a waste of the bitch's season, but it will also put your breeding programme back by at least twelve months.

When you are planning a litter, the first thing you should do is to take a critical look at your bitch. Do not look at her with rose-coloured spectacles; it is essential to be honest with yourself, and look at the bitch objectively. Pick out the faults on your bitch (no, there is no such thing as a perfect specimen), and evaluate her best qualities. A bitch that is to be used for breeding must be sound in mind and body; she must be typical of the breed, with no outstanding faults, and she must be free from hereditary diseases.

Not all countries have the freedom of choice that is available in the UK where there are no restrictions as to how many bitches or dogs a breeder can keep, or how many litters a breeder can breed in any one year. In Switzerland, for example, a breeder may only keep six dogs, and when a breeder wishes to breed a litter, the pedigree of both the sire and dam of the intending litter must be sent to the ruling body. All breeding stock must be free of Progressive Retinal Atrophy (PRA) and Collie Eye Anomaly (CEA) before breeding is allowed, and then an inspector will visit the home where the puppies are to be born to see if the facilities are suitable – only then will the breeder get permission to mate the bitch. When the puppies are born the home will again be inspected to check that the litter is well. In Switzerland Rough and Smooth matings are not allowed.

In Germany the dog or bitch must have a certificate to prove it is worthy of being bred from, and to gain this the Collie must have won a 'Very Good' award three times at shows. If three different judges give the prize 'Good' the bitch may not be bred from. Again, all breeding stock must be clear of any defects such as CEA and PRA and be hip-scored. This is a tall order for any kennel. It is also interesting to note that any dog being exhibited on the continent would not become a Champion if it had missing teeth. The fault is not so severely penalised in the UK. Although these checks mean a tight control is kept on breeding stock, I believe that it limits freedom of choice, and I believe it is this freedom to choose that has produced some of the finest Collies in the world.

FINANCE

Before finally deciding to breed from your bitch, there are a few points which should be taken into consideration. Can you afford a litter of puppies? It is not often that you recoup all you have spent on the enterprise. Check the cost of the stud dog; the fee can be quite substantial, plus travel, and it could mean a day off from work (bitches are never ready on a Sunday!). You should also take into account the cost of the vet, if expert assistance is required. Whelping often takes place during the night, so you may have to call the vet out on an expensive out-of-hours visit. The bitch may have difficulties in whelping and she may need a caesarian, which is another major financial outlay.

You will need to purchase or build a suitable whelping box, and you must have adequate space and facilities for rearing the puppies. It is also advisable to check with your local council, as you may need a breeder's licence if you keep more than one bitch and you are using your home as a breeding establishment. It is important to check that you are the owner of the bitch at the time of mating. Some bitches are sold on breeding terms, and it is important to check all the paperwork so you know what your obligations are. Finally, are you on good terms with your neighbours? Puppies are noisy and can cry quite loudly, even when they are still young, so tell your neighbours of your plans and ask them to bear with you – after all, it is only for a few weeks.

If you have not been put off by all these warnings and you are ready to take the plunge, you will enjoy every second of breeding a litter of puppies. Rough or Smooth, breeding a litter and caring for the puppies is one of life's special pleasures.

CHOOSING A STUD DOG

If you have a Smooth Collie bitch you have a harder task ahead than that which faces the Rough Collie owner. The available gene pool for mating Smooth to Smooth is so small compared with the large numbers of Rough Collie studs available.

The stud dog you choose does not have to be a Champion. Many superbly bred dogs live as family pets or working dogs, and it is well worth searching out these dogs for their valuable bloodlines. In Rough Collie circles this is uncalled for, as the breed has so many good stud dogs available, but for the Smooth breeder who is looking for a mate for a closely line-bred bitch, this source could be a real godsend. There are very few kennels that keep a team of Smooth Collie sires, and over the years I have always tried to place Smooth dogs with local farmers, who are pleased to have a good working easy-to-train dog for a nominal sum, and in this way I have access to these males for stud work when it is needed. Fortunately the Smooth Collie is now becoming much more popular, and hopefully, in time, there will be a more varied gene pool available.

The stud dog you select, whether it is Rough or Smooth, must be sound in mind and body, and he must have a happy outlook on life. Remember that most of your puppies will go to pet homes where temperament will be of the utmost importance. If you are a novice owner it is advisable to seek advice about a potential mate for your bitch. Most breeders are only too happy to help in any way they can. Never be frightened to ask; after all, it is the only way to learn. I remember in my early days I approached Margaret Osborne of the famous Sheil Collies, and I was absolutely terrified! However, Miss Osborne was not only very helpful, she was very kind to me in many ways.

BREEDING PROGRAMMES

The next step is to look for a sire that ties in with the lines of your bitch's pedigree. In fact, there are three types of breeding programmes to consider: line breeding, in breeding, and out crossing.

Line breeding is the mating of dogs who have common relations in the pedigree, and for novice breeders it is the most sensible form of breeding. Line breeding is when both parents have similar bloodlines going back over four or five generations.

In breeding is the mating of close relations such as mother to son, father to daughter, sister to brother. This should only be carried out by experienced breeders who know what faults lie within

Lowerpark Speckleberry: Top Brood 1990, dam of Ch. Lowerpark Moonlighter at Corydon.

Ch. Sandiacre Sweet Lorraine: the only Rough Collie bitch to produce three Champions to three different sires: Ch. Sandiacre Sweet Valentine by Ir. Ch. Sandiacre Strolling, Ch. Sandiacre Stripper by Glenorka Governor General, and Ch. Sandiacre Silence Is Golden by Sangreat Sorrocco.

the pedigree, for as in breeding doubles up on all the good points, it can also double up on bad points too. In breeding cannot produce any new characteristics; it can only produce what is already in the parentage. The main object of in breeding is to fix good points and to eliminate bad ones. It is also used to produce a strain quickly. To in breed, every name on the pedigree should be related, and providing the pedigree contains first-class winning dogs, with no outstanding faults, this type of breeding will produce dogs true to type in size and with distinctive features.

Outcrossing is the mating of unrelated dogs, and seldom produces good stock. Quite often a mating of this kind can produce an outstanding puppy, but this dog or bitch will never breed on. A superb dog produced by outcrossing will not prove to be a good stud dog unless he is mated back to bitches of his own line. Outcrossing can be useful when a serious fault comes into a breed. An outcross dog or bitch can be mated back to the best line on the pedigree, and the resulting puppies should then be in bred to produce the strain you wish to obtain.

SOME MATINGS THAT PRODUCE GOOD STOCK

Providing the stock you are using has no major faults some of the best matings are: grandfather to grand-daughter, grandmother to grandson, and half-brother to half-sister. A full brother-sister mating is not really worth doing as the puppies will never be better than the parents. Uncle to niece, and aunt to nephew can be successful, and, if you are really sure of your pedigree, mating father to daughter can produce some outstanding results. However, this type of breeding is only for the experienced breeders. In all instances the most important aspect of breeding to bear in mind is that a good brood bitch is worth more than gold.

The choice is further complicated if you are breeding to produce a particular colour (see Chapter Seven: Colours of the Collie). The sire you choose should not have outstanding faults, and it should not double up on the bitch's weak points. Never use a dog with prick ears – in fact, you should not be breeding from a bitch that has prick ears. I cannot tolerate a Collie, Rough or Smooth, with prick ears – I believe it is one of the worst faults the breed can possess. The Collie, Rough and Smooth, should still be bred on working lines, so watch out for faults such as weak feet and straight shoulders, which are very hard to breed out. You should also ask to see the stud dog's certificates stating that he is clear of Progressive Retinal Atrophy (PRA) and Collie Eye Anomaly (CEA). PRA is now almost unheard of in the Rough and Smooth Collie, but CEA is quite common in all Collie breeds.

Sometimes the best show bitches do not make the best mothers, so if you want to develop your breeding programme, it is useful to keep a few well-bred bitches of impeccable breeding. These bitches will play a vital role in keeping your kennel to the fore while you are busy showing the 'stars' of the kennel. It always amazes me when people around the show ring ask about a dog's sire after a big win. They seem to forget that the dog in question also had a mother, who must have been equally influential. In fact, I think that a brood bitch is far more important to a breeder than any dog, for if you have a good bitch you can use any of the best dogs in the country. So do make sure that the bitches do you justice, and your kennel will earn you a reputation for breeding good, sound stock.

THE IN-SEASON BITCH

Before your bitch comes into season, you must check that she has been wormed; she should be in tip-top condition, and all her inoculations should be up to date. Most bitches are a week coming on heat, a week on heat, and a week going off. You must watch your bitch carefully during this time to decide what day she will be ready for mating. Some bitches will stand within a few days of coming on heat, and with this type you are never really sure if the bitch has conceived or not. However, most bitches will stand for a dog between the tenth and fifteenth day. Having said that, all bitches are different, and so it is a matter of judging when your bitch is ready.

It is easy to asses this if you own a male, as the bitch will start flirting with the dog as soon as she is ready – if she is not ready she may well take off his head! When a bitch is receptive the vulva swells and goes soft, and the blood colour will have changed to a pale watery discharge. When the vulva becomes very soft you will find the bitch is at her most receptive, and this applies to any male who takes her fancy – even the mongrel down the road!

LEADING BROODS

Many speak of leading sires, but every dog has a mother, and one of the most prolific brood bitches was the beautiful Ch. Rifflesea Reward of Glenmist, bred by Dr and Mrs Collins (nee Hazel Hunt). This outstanding sable and white bitch was worth her weight in gold to her owner, Frank Mitchell. While obtaining her titles of Obedience and Show Champion she whelped three litters, producing four Champion daughters: Ch. Sapphire of Glenmist, Ch. Sceptre of Glenmist, Ch. Spellbinder of Glenmist and Ch. Starlet of Glenmist. Ch. Starlet produced Ch. Larkena Vanara Golden Victor. Ch. Sapphire produced two Champion males, Ch. Glenmist Golden Legacy and Ch. Pattingham Gay Legend of Glenmist, both sired by Ch. Debonair of Glenmist, and two female Champions, Ch. Lovely Lady of Glenmist and Ch. Pattingham Gay Lady of Glenmist, sired by the tricolour dog, Rifflesea Royalist.

Chapter Sixteen

PREGNANCY AND WHELPING

CARE DURING PREGNANCY

The weeks leading up to the whelping date are crucial and great care must be taken of your bitch at this time. For the first few weeks after the mating you do not need to do anything different as your bitch may not even be pregnant. All bitches vary in character, and the first sign that your bitch is in whelp may be a slight change in her behaviour. You will obviously detect this more quickly if your Collie is a house dog rather than a kennel dog. A few weeks after mating, the in-whelp bitch will thicken over the loin, her nipples will become more erect and swollen, and she will constantly stop to lick herself.

When you are sure your bitch is in whelp you must pay particular attention to diet, as she requires nourishment for her unborn puppies as well as for herself. From the fourth week, increase the intake of food to a light breakfast consisting of any type of cereal, plus milk. It is important to add a supplement of calcium every day, and I find it easier to remember if I add this to the breakfast meal. At midday feed normal rations, but if possible, buy some good-quality fresh mince from the butcher. In the evening feed a small supper of your bitch's favourite food – and you will find this is ample for a bitch in whelp. Do not over-feed, or you will end up with very fat bitch, who may have difficulty whelping. At the fifth week some bitches go off their food completely, so you must be patient and try to find something to tempt her appetite, such as chicken or rabbit. Do not let your bitch become too choosy, as Collies can be very cunning and will play on your sympathy.

At this stage the bitch will start to show, very slightly, that she is in whelp. She will appear to have sprung her ribs, giving an almost pear shape to her figure. By seven weeks she will really have thickened all over, and she will look overloaded on the front (forechest). She will start bagging up, i.e. her teats will be much larger and quite often the hair around the teats will have very nearly disappeared – this is nature's way of clearing the area where the pups will suckle. Apart from monitoring these changes, and keeping your bitch well-fed and clean, you should allow her to carry on her life as normal.

As the day draws near you must begin to make preparations for whelping. You must first decide where your bitch should whelp. This should be a quiet place, away from the hurly-burly of the household. No bitch should be expected to whelp in a busy kitchen or in a hallway. At least a week before the due date you should get the whelping quarters ready, so the the bitch has a chance to get used to the new environment. There are a number of purpose-built whelping boxes on the market, but if you do not want to invest in one of these, a large box can be constructed. This should have ample room for the bitch to turn herself round, and she should be able to stretch out in comfort.

It is important that the whelping quarters are warm (approximately 70 degrees Fahrenheit), and they must be draught-free. I always use a heated pad, in preference to an infra-red lamp. Many breeders swear by lamps, but I have found that it is easy for the bitch to get over-heated if she is subjected to an overhead lamp that she cannot move away from. The fleecy man-made washable material provides excellent bedding, and the puppies will retain all their body heat if this is used. Never use straw or hay; it is most unsuitable for a bitch and puppies.

As the day draws near it is advisable to start taking your bitch's temperature twice daily. The average temperature for a dog is 101 degrees Fahrenheit, but twenty-four hours before whelping, a bitch's temperature will usually drop to about 98 degrees. At this time the bitch will want to pass water more frequently, and she will become increasingly restless. When this happens it is advisable to take the bitch to her whelping quarters. At this stage most bitches will scratch up their bedding, constantly remaking their bed in preparation for whelping. It is best to leave the bitch alone, checking on her at regular intervals. It is important to adopt a calm, quiet manner in order to give the bitch confidence.

If your bitch is a Rough Collie make sure all her fur is out of the way. Tie back the petticoats or, better still, cut them off. I always bandage up the tail, as the hanging fur will get wet and soiled, and it can be very dangerous if a puppy is caught up in a strand of fur – it is all too easy for a newborn puppy to strangle in this situation.

THE WHELPING

ITEMS REQUIRED FOR WHELPING

A bowl of warm water (for washing your hands).
Savlon (to put into the water to make sure everything is antiseptic).
Sterile scissors for cutting the cord or, if possible, artery forceps.
Liquid calcium.
Permanganate of Potash (available from the pharmacist). This quells bleeding if the bitch bites an umbilical cord too short.
Disposable gloves.
Paper towelling (kitchen rolls).
Kitchen scales (for weighing the newborn puppies).
A cardboard box and a wrapped hot-water bottle, in case you need to transfer the puppies to the vet, in the event of complications.

STAGES OF LABOUR

Twenty-four hours before she is due, the bitch's temperature will drop to around 98 degrees Fahrenheit. The lips of the vagina soften and protrude. As the time draws near, the bitch will become increasingly restless; she will pant heavily and constantly lick her vulva. She will go to her bed and scratch up newspaper or bedding frantically. She will usually refuse all food. This stage can last from a couple of hours to twenty-four hours.

As the bitch moves into the next stage of her labour, the heavy panting will change to contractions, and the bitch will tremble and look glazed about the eyes. The cervix will now be dilating, and quite often a clear watery discharge can be seen. As the labour pains get under way, the bitch will pant a great deal and become very restless. As the contractions become stronger, the bitch will arch her back – there may be twenty to thirty minutes between each contraction, with the

Stages of whelping

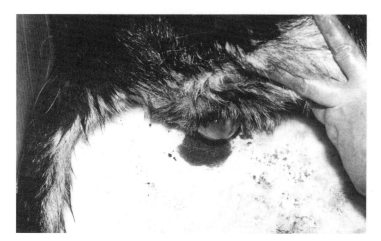

First glimpse of the water bag, which has the appearance of a skin-like bulb.

A pup still in the sac.

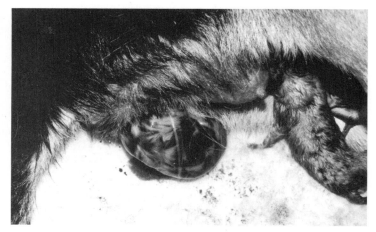

bitch pushing and straining harder with each contraction. As whelping commences you will see a pale-green watery discharge staining the bed – this is quite normal. The water bag is the first thing to be seen; it appears as a skin-like bulb. In the case of a protracted labour, every time the bitch pushes down, the bag emerges, and then it may disappear and reappear a few times. Do not, at this stage, touch the water sac, as the fluid inside the bag is protecting the puppy from outside pressure. When the membrane bursts, it is usually followed by a puppy, nose-first. If everything is proceeding normally your bitch will tear the sac herself, letting out the fluid and almost immediately the puppy will emerge, attached to the placenta and umbilical cord. If your bitch is a maiden, she may well be surprised at what is happening and she may not know what to do next. In this instance you must very carefully help the bitch by tearing the sac with finger and thumb – never attempt to cut this sac.

As the puppy emerges the bitch will take over and bite the cord. If the bitch gets carried away

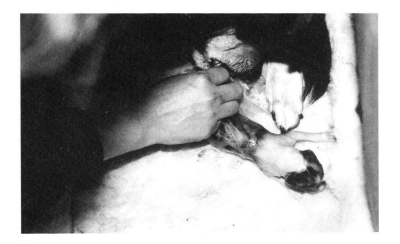

The puppy still attached to the placenta. The bitch chews the cord to sever herself from the puppy.

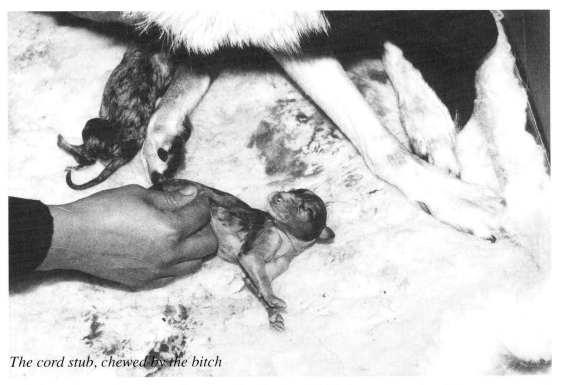

The cord stub, chewed by the bitch

and chews the cord too short, there may be bleeding. If this happens, apply a little permanganate of potash on the stump, using a cotton bud, and the bleeding will stop instantly. If, on the other hand the bitch is reluctant to bite the cord you will have to do it for her, and this is where your sterile scissors come into use. If you do not have a steriliser (such as a Milton), you can immerse the scissors in surgical spirit. Make sure the potash powder is to hand in case of heavy bleeding.

Sever the cord about two inches from the body of the pup and apply the potash crystals. If at all possible, use artery forceps instead of scissors, as with forceps you do not need to cut the cord so abruptly, you just squash the forceps together and tear off the end of the placenta.

Most mothers will constantly lick the new-born whelp, but again, if the bitch does not appear to know what to do, you must take over. First, make sure there is no mucus in the mouth. Then hold it out for the bitch to see, and if she still fails to respond, you must gently rub the puppy with soft towels or kitchen roll. This will stimulate the puppy and make it cry out. At this stage the bitch usually realises what is expected of her; her maternal instincts will take over and she will probably finish whelping with no extra assistance. However, she should never be left unsupervised in case any problems arise. Many bitches like to eat the placenta (afterbirth), and quite often the bitch will get to it before you have a chance to dispose of it. This does not harm the bitch in any way; it is nature's way of providing nourishment for the bitch. The only trouble is that they work as a laxative, and it is therefore preferable if the bitch does not eat all the placentas.

It is quite usual for puppies to be born breech, i.e. feet-first. However, this can be be very exhausting for your bitch if it slows up the delivery, so you must try to help if you feel you can – if not, you should call your vet. To assist your bitch, first scrub your hands, and then, as the bitch pushes hard, very gently put fingers from both hands inside the vulva. Then, as the bitch pushes, you will be able to hold on to the little body to prevent it going in again. With each push, gently ease the puppy out.

Pups may be born at varying intervals – anything from five minutes to thirty minutes is perfectly normal. Sometimes when a few pups have been born the bitch will lie quiet; this probably signals the halfway mark because the uterus is made up of two separate horns and when one horn is empty the other takes over. This does not mean that both sides carry the same number of puppies; sometimes a bitch will have five pups in one horn and only one or two in the other. You will know when the bitch is going to start up again as she will start to have contractions again.

Do not fuss around the bitch too much; just stay with her, encouraging her and talking to her calmly, and hopefully all will proceed smoothly. Some bitches whelp very quickly, while others take hours. During the whelping, offer your bitch some cold milk and glucose to drink. Sometimes puppies are born very quickly and no help is needed, but if, after continued straining, nothing has happened then it advisable to call for the vet. It is important to inform your vet when a litter is due, so that he is prepared for a call-out if complications arise. Collies, Rough and Smooth, are normally very easy whelpers. All should go well, but you must be prepared for an emergency. A car that starts first time is a must, and you should make arrangements with a fellow breeder, so that someone is available if a helping hand is required.

When your bitch has finished whelping, you will need to clean her up thoroughly and lay down clean bedding. It takes no time to wash the Smooth Collie bitch, using a cloth with warm water. The task is far more difficult with a Rough Collie as her petticoats could be stained with the green discharge, and every last trace must be washed away, and then she must be dried. This job is important, not only to avoid a foul smell, but also because the puppies could get caught up in any wet fur and strangle. While you are doing this, you can run your eye over the newborn pups to see if any defects are evident.

Some breeders like to weigh their pups as they are born, so that they can see how they progress over the first few days – kitchen scales are perfectly adequate for this. Maiden bitches do not always have milk, but they will start to produce when stimulated by the suckling of the pups. If you have a puppy that does not suckle at first, check to see if it has a cleft palate. If all is well, try to get the puppy on to the teat by holding its head, and then, using thumb and first finger, gently open the mouth and attach the pup to the teat. If this fails and the puppy is a sickly one, you will have to bottle-feed.

WHELPING COMPLICATIONS

If you think, at any stage, that the bitch is having problems, it is most important to telephone the vet immediately. In this instance it does not matter if it is the middle of the night; if you wait until morning it could well be too late, and you may be risking your bitch's life as well as that of the unborn puppies. Complications can arise, even with the most experienced breeder, so make sure you have the vet's telephone number to hand.

The signs to look for are inertia, which is when labour pains cease and the bitch has produced nothing. This can be caused by a hormone deficiency or by sheer exhaustion from a long labour. Sometimes a bitch may have a congenital fault which prevents her whelping. It could be that the bitch's pelvis is too small to pass a puppy, or it could be that a puppy is too large to pass. Sometimes a puppy may have passed through the birth canal and the head may even be felt, but if the bitch is too exhausted to push, or if she pushes to no avail, you must inform the vet straightaway. Sometimes the water bag bursts and there is no sign of a puppy, and so a caesarian section will need to be carried out. The most common cause for a caesarian is an overlarge puppy or one in the wrong position.

If an emergency arises, the first thing you must do is telephone the surgery. If you are calling at night, you will probably be asked to wait while your call is put through to the vet on night duty. It is important to tell the vet exactly what is happening, so you must remain calm and answer any questions as clearly and accurately as possible. The vet will come to your house, but it will save time if you take the bitch and newborn puppies (if she has already produced some) to the surgery in case a caesarian is required. Place the puppies in a box with a covered hot-water bottle; it is essential that they do not loose body heat. While all this is going on, you must constantly reassure the bitch so that she does not become too upset.

POST-WHELPING

Most bitches will refuse to leave a newborn litter, and I never make my bitches go out unless they want to – I find they will usually go out when the need arises. When a bitch is nursing a litter, never put her out with your other dogs as the excitement could result in the loss of her milk. It is also essential that she has a good intake of calcium to avoid the risk of eclampsia. (See Chapter Eighteen: Health Care.)

For the first twenty-four hours do not give the dam a heavy meal, as she is lying down most of the time and a full stomach will make her feel uncomfortable. I find that most bitches will be tempted by milky cereals, or scrambled eggs and brown bread. At this post-whelping stage your bitch should have light, nourishing food, and this should be divided into four medium-sized meals a day. Your bitch has done her best for you, presenting you with a litter of contented puppies, and you must now do your best for her, giving her all the care and attention you can.

Chapter Seventeen

REARING

THE FIRST DAYS

The first few days after whelping are vital both to pups and mother. You must check every few hours to see all is well, making sure the puppies are all suckling and none are being pushed off the milk bar. It is very important that the puppies are kept warm. When you enter the whelping room you should hear suckling noises, with the occasional cry from a puppy that has been pushed off the milk bar. Some puppies also cry out when the dam pushes them around when she is cleaning them.

If any of the puppies is making a constant mewing noise, you must check to see that all is well. Some puppies are very greedy from birth and they will push the smaller ones out of the way at feeding time. If you are worried about a puppy, take it away from the bitch so you can examine it more closely. It may be weak and suffering from the cold. If this is the case you can wrap the pup in a warm towel. Many a puppy has been revived by placing it on a plate in a warm oven with the door wide open; of course, great care must be taken at all times when carrying out this survival operation.

When the puppies are three days old, you must decide if you want the vet to remove the dew claws. You are not obliged to have this done, it is a matter of personal preference.

In these first few days, I leave the bitch to do most of the work, just ensuring that everything is going smoothly and that the whelping box is kept fresh and clean. In all my years as a breeder, I have never got over the excitement of a new litter of puppies, Rough and Smooth alike – I am lost for words at the sheer marvel of it all.

HAND REARING

There may be circumstances when your bitch is unable to feed the litter. She may be an indifferent mother, she may have too many puppies to feed, or she may be taken ill and be unable to fulfil her maternal duties. Occasionally a mother may die during whelping or during a caesarean operation, and then you will have orphan puppies to rear.

Tube-feeding is one method of feeding newborn puppies, but this is potentially dangerous, particularly for the novice breeder. It is all too easy to get fluid on to the lungs, and this can prove fatal. If you choose this method, you should ask your vet for special advice. Bottle-feeding is a much simpler solution. There are a number of specially designed feeding bottles available, and all countries have some form of bottle suitable for feeding orphan puppies. If an animal bottle cannot be found, you can use a human baby bottle, but take care the hole in the teat is not too big for a tiny pup. You can buy teats with no holes, and so you can make the hole the size you require. For a tiny puppy, a hole made with a safety pin would suffice, and this hole may be made bigger as the

A well-cared for litter of Smooth Collies, with all the puppies looking clean, comfortable and well-fed.

Sunsweet Rough Collie puppies, pictured at six weeks.

puppy grows. I always hold the tip of the pin over a flame to make sure that the tip is warm, and this way it is easier to make the hole.

When I am feeding a tiny newborn pup, I always hold the puppy in an upright position enclosing the puppy in the whole of my hand. In this way the puppy will feel secure and will not wriggle. Gently open pup's mouth with the finger and thumb of the one hand, and gently nuzzle the teat into the mouth. Make sure that you follow the manufacturer's instructions when you are measuring out the quantity of milk replacer to use, and also as to how often you feed.
A Collie, Rough or Smooth, is classed as a medium breed and quantities should be:
Birth to seven days: 5 to 6ml. every two hours.
Eight to fourteen days: 10 to 12ml. every three hours.

As the puppy grows you increase the quantity, but decrease the number of feeds, e.g. twenty-two to twenty-eight days: 25ml. every four hours, and five times daily. By the time a puppy is twenty-eight days old it should be having small amounts of minced meat, followed by a drink of milk replacer. As soon as possible try to get orphan pups to lap; some will start as early as three weeks of age. However, feeding, on its own, is not enough. You must keep puppies warm and comfortable, and this entails 'topping and tailing'. When you have fed the puppies you must make them go to the toilet. The mother would normally stimulate the puppy by licking its rear end. In the absence of the mother you must take a little cotton wool that has been dipped lightly in a little warm olive oil, and, very lightly, make a circular motion on the tummy until the puppy has emptied its bowels and passed water. The puppy will then have to be cleaned using warm water, and then dusted with baby powder.

WEANING
Both Rough and Smooth Collies are very good doers, and weaning is a very easy task. I find that Smooths take to solids earlier than the Roughs, and certainly the Smooth Collie is far easier to keep clean during the weaning process. Most puppies wander merrily through a tray of milky weetabix or porridge, and a lack of fur is definitely an advantage for the breeder!

We are lucky in being able to pick and choose what food to give our dogs, and there are many very good products on the market, all containing the minerals and vitamins that young stock needs. However, I always start my puppies off, whether they are Rough or Smooth, by using the same method that I have used for the last twenty years. It has always given me good results, so I see no reason to change.

I start weaning my puppies at just under three weeks if it is a large litter, but no matter the size of litter, I always make sure the puppies have had their first taste of meat by the time they are three weeks old. I use top-quality butcher's minced beef, and grind it to a pulp. This can be taken quite readily from a small spoon, and I offer each puppy one spoonful, three times a day. By the time the puppies are five weeks old, I feed minced beef mixed with a little weetabix three times a day. It is important to feed the puppies when they are hungry, and allow them to suckle once they have eaten their solids.

As the puppies increase in size, I add a meal of well-soaked puppy biscuit, with meat or tripe. You will find that by adding weetabix to the mince while the puppies are very young, the bowel movement will always be firm and you will have no scouring problems. I then slowly introduce my puppies to a complete diet. I use a product that contains no soya, as most dogs find this hard to digest. By the time the puppies are seven weeks old a typical day's intake of food would be:

BREAKFAST: milk and cereal, such as porridge, weetabix or bran flakes.

Weaning should be undertaken gradually, so that mother and puppies remain contented.

A litter of Rough Collie puppies at eight weeks, fully weaned and ready to go to new homes.

LUNCH: Either well-soaked biscuit and meat, tripe, or any puppy tinned food. All the puppy diets on the market are well balanced, and you choose the one that suits your needs.
TEA: As above, but you may alternate with scrambled eggs, fish or chicken.
SUPPER: A milky supper, or well-soaked puppy biscuit, or complete diet.

From eight to twelve weeks your puppy should eat at least four good, nourishing meals a day. I believe you only get out what you put in, and to build a show dog you need the best food and care you can give. Until your puppy is ten months old it should have three meals a day, and from ten months feed a small breakfast and an evening meal.

WORMING

It is most important that you worm your puppies, as they will probably be infested with roundworms (see Chapter Eighteen: Health Care). The vet will recommend a suitable product that is palatable and easy to use. I worm my puppies weekly until they are eight weeks old, and then fortnightly until four months of age. Thereafter, I worm all my dogs every three months for roundworm, and I give a total wormer once a year.

PUPPY CARE

While rearing your litter, Rough or Smooth, great care must be taken at all times to keep the puppies clean and dry. If the litter is born in winter then warmth will be of the utmost importance. If the litter is to be reared in a kennel, it must be draught-free and cosy. Collie puppies are very quick to learn, and if paper is laid down away from the actual bed they will soon become clean. Collies will never foul the bed they sleep in, as long as they have access to a toilet area.

If it is warm enough to allow your puppies outside, make sure that the ground is fairly dry. Under no circumstances, should you put a wet puppy to bed without first drying it thoroughly. Here, Smooths have the advantage, as a quick rub-down is all that is needed. It is also important to bear in mind that the Smooth does not have the thick woolly coat of the Rough, so make sure the puppies are warm as toast in the bed.

LEAVING HOME

Make sure that the puppy's pedigree is ready to hand over to the new owners, and always give a diet sheet to a novice owner. I find the best age for a puppy to go to its new home is around eight weeks, but every breeder has their own ideas. At eight weeks a puppy will soon settle away from its litter mates; if a pup is older it will find it harder to adapt and will often cry and go off its food for a few days. This is because the pup is used to competing for its food with its littermates, and it is suddenly at a loss when it is presented with a whole bowl of food to itself.

Chapter Eighteen

HEALTH CARE

GENERAL CARE

Collies, Rough and Smooth, are a very healthy breed, and some can go through life without ever having to go to the vet, except for routine vaccinations. A healthy diet is the key to general well being, and if you want to keep a Collie in show condition, it is essential to provide a good, balanced diet. I feed a varied diet with plenty of roughage, including raw carrots, which my Collies love to chew on. Protein is provided in the meat content, and white meats (such as chicken and fish) and eggs are also very nourishing. I also feed tripe mixed with a good brand of wholemeal biscuit.

Neither Rough or Smooth Collies need to be pampered, but all dogs need a place of their own to lie in. On no account let your Collie go to its bed if it is still wet after going out in the rain or the snow. First, rub the dog down well with a warm, dry towel. It is a good idea to keep a dry towel within easy reach of the Collie's sleeping quarters.

Rough and Smooth Collies very seldom get ear problems, due to the fact they have a semi-erect ear carriage, rather than Spaniel-type ears, which are more prone to problems. However, if your Collie is shaking its head a lot, or rubbing its ears, you should clean them with a little warm water and cotton wool. Never poke about in your Collie's ears; not only is it dangerous, but it usually pushes the rubbish further down into the ear canal, causing infection. Most vets provide ear-cleaning material; this is usually in the form of a very mild antiseptic that will remove all debris at the base of the ear, and will leave the ear clean and sweet-smelling.

All dog owners should keep a small medicine cabinet for general use and for emergencies. This should be checked every year, and any unused medicines or creams that are out of date should be thrown away. The medicine cabinet should contain:

Aspirin or Dispirin: To be used with great care, first seeking advice from your vet.
Eye drops.
Calcium: All young stock need some form of calcium, and it is an important supplement for the in-whelp and nursing bitch.
Savlon: To use as an antiseptic on cuts.
Flea powder or spray.
Glucose: This is a good source of energy, and is most useful for the whelping bitch, and for dogs that are unwell and not able to take solid food,
Honey: This is very useful for sore throats after a bout of kennel cough.
Kaolin Poultice. This is useful for relieving inflammation, and it is godsend for 'flying ear' problems. When puppies begin teething, apply a little kaolin poultice on the extreme tip of the ear, and this helps to weight the ear down and keep the fold. It can stay on as long as you like, and it is very easy to remove with a little surgical spirit.
Milk of Magnesia: This is a good standby for

upset stomachs.

Olive oil: This is useful for hand-rearing orphan puppies. Put a little warmed olive oil on cotton wool, and you can then stimulate a puppy to go to the toilet.

Vaseline: This is handy at mating time; a little inserted in the bitch's vagina can make all the difference to getting an easy mating with a maiden bitch.

Worming tablets.

Cotton wool.

Sterile swabs.

Bandages.

A roll of plaster.

Nail clippers.

DOGS AND BITCHES

If your Collie is a bitch, she should be closely observed at season times, to make sure that her cycle is following a normal pattern. She should also be examined for any lumps around her teats; mammary tumours that are caught early can be removed. Any discharge after a season should be looked upon with grave concern and must be checked by your vet. If you keep stud dogs, Rough or Smooth, regular checks should be made for any discharge from the penis, and for any sign of testicular tumours.

ADMINISTERING LIQUID MEDICINE

First, read the instructions on the label, and make sure that you measure out the exact dose. The standard dosage is either 5mls or 10mls. Some dogs are co-operative about swallowing medicines from a spoon, but if you have a dog that is very stubborn, ask your vet to provide you with a syringe. The medicine can be sucked up (again, ensuring that you have the correct dosage); then insert the end of the syringe in the Collie's mouth; depress plunger, and hold the mouth shut for a few seconds – the operation it is over and done with, in no time at all.

ADMINISTERING TABLETS

Pills and capsules are much easier to administer, as you can hide them in a tasty titbit. I always use cheese for this purpose, which is a titbit that few Collies can resist. However, there is always the awkward dog who insists on spitting out the pill or capsule, no matter how well it is disguised. In this instance, you will need to open the dog's mouth, using your finger and thumb, and place the pill at the very back of the dog's throat. Close the mouth, and wait a second so that you are certain that the pill has been swallowed.

TAKING YOUR COLLIE'S TEMPERATURE

Always use a blunt-ended thermometer. Shake it down well, and grease the end with a little lubricating jelly or Vaseline. Insert the end of the thermometer into the rectum for at least one minute; you can rotate the thermometer so that you can watch for the mercury to rise. Remove thermometer and take a reading; the average temperature for a dog is 101.4. degrees Fahrenheit. This drops to 98F at the time of whelping; any other change in temperature should be closely watched. Clean the end of the thermometer with clean cotton wool, and keep it in a safe place.

NURSING A SICK DOG

Collies are notoriously hardy, and are easy to care for, but if you keep several Collies or you start breeding with your dogs, the chances of having a sick animal are bound to increase. Here are a few hints to make the task easier for Collie and owner.

It is most important to put the ailing dog in a nice, quiet room with low light or a night-light. Make sure the room is warm and free from draughts. Keep the bedding, and the Collie, scrupulously clean. Nursing a sick Collie is very time-consuming, so the 'sick room' should be located as conveniently as possible, so that you can carry on with other household jobs, while still being on hand for your Collie.

It is a good idea to adopt a daily routine of cleaning away any discharge from your Collie's eyes or nose, and gently wiping its face and mouth with a clean flannel. If the dog's nose is dry, rub in a little baby oil. If your Collie is really ill, it will need to be turned from one side to the other every few hours, and at the same time you can make sure that the bedding is comfortable. I find the fleecy bedding, which allows moisture to soak through, is invaluable when nursing sick Collies, or very old dogs. It is so soft, and yet it is very easy to wash and dry quickly.

If your Collie refuses food, do not try to force feed. However, you must ensure that it takes in fluids. If the dog will not drink readily, then you must use a syringe or dropper, gently letting the liquid into the side of the mouth, a little at a time. An electrolyte solution is the best form of fluid, as this will prevent your Collie from dehydrating. Medicines and tablets should be given at the exact times stated on the medicine labels.

Collies are sensitive animals and respond to the mood of their owners, so try not to fuss too much. Just make sure the Collie is as comfortable as possible, and try to spend a little time sitting with your dog and keeping it company during the course of the day.

POST-OPERATIVE CARE

If your Collie has to undergo surgery at any time in its life, it will need special care to help it recuperate from its operation. When you collect your Collie from the surgery after an operation, it should be able to walk out; most vets will not allow a dog to go home if it is still wobbly on its legs. When you get home, the Collie should be kept quiet, in a warm place. It should be kept away from other dogs in the house, never left in a kennel, as you will not be able to keep a close watch on it.

Your Collie will not want to eat much for the first few days after surgery, so it is advisable to make a light, tasty meal instead of the usual diet. Chicken, fish, or scrambled eggs, with a little brown bread or rice, has a high protein content and is very easy to digest. Offer little meals, instead of one big meal. The stomach should never be over-loaded, especially if the operation was internal. As far as fluids are concerned, let your Collie drink little and often, rather than letting it fill up with water.

Do not wash surgery wounds; this prevents healing and may let in infection. Once the wound is clean and dry, it should be left to heal. Your Collie should be closely observed at all times to ensure that it does not lick the wound, or try to remove the stitches. After ten days, the stitches will be removed by your vet, who will check to see that all is well. Most Collies seem to have amazing powers of recovery, and within a few days of surgery they are up and about, as if nothing had happened. However, for the first few days, you must prevent your Collie from jumping up on to beds, and from going up and down stairs. A little light exercise is all that is required, as this prevents any clots from forming. If you detect any swelling or redness around the wound, this must be reported to your vet straightaway.

INOCULATIONS

All Collies should have up-to-date inoculations against the following diseases: distemper, hepatitis, leptospirosis, parvovirus and kennel cough. Most vets will vaccinate a puppy from the age of ten weeks (some a little earlier at the owner's request). The first vaccine consists of leptospirosis and hepatitis, followed two weeks later with a second dose of leptospirosis, hepatitis, plus distemper and parvovirus. You may, if you wish, have one of the newer vaccines on the market that include kennel cough. A week after the second injection your puppy is ready to face the world, protected from all major infections. It is advisable to have a yearly booster and most vets send out reminders to this effect.

DISTEMPER

Although Distemper is quite rare now that good vaccines are on the market, there have been a few outbreaks. The virus affects many tissues including the respiratory and gastrointestinal regions, and also the nervous systems. In unvaccinated dogs the signs are high temperature, nasal and ocular discharge, vomiting and also diarrhoea, followed by dehydration, If left untreated this disease is fatal. It affects the nervous system with 'Chorea', which causes involuntary movement (twitching of the limbs and other groups of muscles even when the dog is sleeping). At present there is no specific cure for distemper, but with good therapy, secondary infections can be prevented. Supportive therapy includes antibiotics, fluids and round-the-clock nursing care. Although the prognosis is very grave, a few dogs have recovered fully. Full vaccinations followed by yearly boosters will prevent your Collie becoming infected.

INFECTIOUS CANINE HEPATITIS

This is a highly contagious disease, not to be confused with the human form of hepatitis. Early signs are a loss of appetite, high temperature, vomiting and diarrhoea. The gums turn very pale and jaundice often occurs. If left untreated, your Collie will deteriorate rapidly, so do seek veterinary advice promptly.

LEPTOSPIRA CANICOLA

This disease is often picked up by allowing your Collie to sniff where other dogs have urinated. The signs are similar to hepatitis, and if left untreated it can cause permanent damage to the kidneys. This is also a highly contagious disease, and great care must be taken when treating an affected animal, as this infection can be transmitted to humans, so do take care and seek veterinary advice.

LEPTOSPIROSIS ICTEROHAEMORRHAGIAE

This disease is highly dangerous, as it can be passed on to humans. The bacteria are transmitted by rat urine on the ground, and are often around dogs' outdoor drinking bowls, and even windfall fruit. So if your Collie has an outside kennel and run, it is advisable to take up its drinking bowl every night to avoid possible contamination. Runs and kennels should be thoroughly scrubbed as a matter of routine, but particularly in the winter months when rats are looking for a place to nest. A dog with this disease will suffer from severe thirst, a high temperature, diarrhoea, vomiting, and it will have a frequent need to pass urine. The dog will also experience pain, and jaundice and total apathy set in very quickly, so it is vital to seek veterinary assistance.

CANINE PARVOVIRUS

This is a relatively new virus to affect dogs, and it has a very short incubation period of five to seven days. The virus is excreted in faeces, and it is very difficult to eradicate. The virus can be transmitted from clothes and shoes that have been in contact with the disease. The common parvo infection can affect a Collie at any age, and in the very young it can be fatal. Signs to watch for are refusal of food and water, protracted vomiting, pain, and diarrhoea with a high blood content. A tell-tale sign is a most offensive smell.

CANINE PARVOVIRUS MYOCARDITIS

This occurs when the whelping bitch has had no protection against the disease, and the resulting litter will carry no protection. The puppies show no signs of ill health, and then at four to eight weeks they may collapse and die, because the heart is weakened by the disease. An entire litter of healthy pups will be affected and they are all likely to die. If any do survive, they may well die of a heart attack later on life.

In order to prevent this terrible disaster, it is essential that your Collie bitch is well vaccinated before she is due to be mated. Once the disease invades your premises it is very hard to eradicate the virus, as it can get into the earth. One of the best disinfectants to use is a strong household bleach. Canine Parvovirus Myocarditis had devastating effects when it first came to the UK, but, thankfully, it is now far less common.

With more and more dogs now being vaccinated, the possibility of your Collie catching these diseases is now much rarer, but never become complacent. Always keep your Collie's boosters up to date, and then you will not have to face the heartache of losing your stock.

KENNEL COUGH

Some Collies never have kennel cough, while others may be plagued with it every year. Dogs that stay in boarding kennels or visit dog shows in the summer months are prone to catching kennel cough, as the disease is transmitted from dog to dog where animals meet together in close proximity. As humans catch colds and flu by being in contact with people who have a cold or flu, so dogs become infected by breathing in infected airborne particles.

The signs are a protracted cough – sometimes the noise is like a dog trying to clear its throat. Most dogs are not affected too severely by this, but very old dogs and very young puppies should be treated promptly by a vet. Like most viral illnesses you can only treat the symptoms, and usually a seven-day course of broad spectrum antibiotics will clear up the problem. A little honey is very soothing for the dog with kennel cough, and so is a spoonful of children's Benylin cough syrup, which eases the sore throat from constant coughing. Most dogs, if they are otherwise healthy, will still continue to be bright and alert, and will eat as normal.

If kennel cough breaks out among your Collies, you must isolate the affected animals from the unaffected until recovery is complete, and stay away from all dog shows and training groups. Ask your vet for a kennel cough vaccine – most vets now incorporate a kennel cough vaccine with the yearly booster.

PARASITES

ENDOPARASITES

These live within the body, and there are a number of types which most commonly affect dogs.

ROUNDWORM (Toxocara Canis): This parasite is three to five inches long, and pointed at both ends. The roundworm larvae lie dormant in the bitch, but when she becomes pregnant, the larvae will migrate to the uterus and into the unborn puppies. That is why *all* puppies have roundworms. By the time the pups are a few weeks old, the worms will be at the adult stage. Puppies that are 'wormy' will have diarrhoea and a poor, harsh coat. Badly affected puppies will have a pot belly, and they will be slow to grow. If puppies are wormed at regular intervals this need never occur. The bitch should be wormed before she is mated, and the pups should be wormed as early as three weeks. The vet will be able to supply you with a liquid wormer, which is easy to administer. Thereafter, the puppies should be wormed every two weeks until they are twelve weeks old, then every four months for the rest their lives.

TAPEWORM (Dipylidium Caninum): A Collie that is kept free from fleas rarely suffers from this parasite, as the flea acts as the intermediate host. A Collie that is infested will lose condition and will probably have a depraved appetite. The tapeworm migrates into the small intestine and is very long, sometimes longer than twenty inches. These worms are very noticeable; they resemble rice grains, and stick to the fur around the anus and can sometimes be seen on the dog's bedding.

Fleas play a vital role in spreading tapeworm. The fleas, which are visible to the naked eye, are reddish-brown in colour, and they feed on the dog's blood. Like all insects, they have several stages in their life cycle. The flea sucks the blood, and then lays its eggs in the dog's bedding, in carpets, and in soft furnishings. When your Collie kills and eats a flea, the worm heads are released into the intestine and mature into adult tapeworms. When the eggs hatch into larvae, deep in soft carpets and furnishings, they feed on dust, and within a short time the larvae forms a cocoon. In less than fifteen days the flea emerges to start the cycle all over again. One flea can lay up to five-hundred eggs in a lifetime. The tapeworm itself produces thousands of eggs in each tiny segment, and the flea feeds off these eggs.

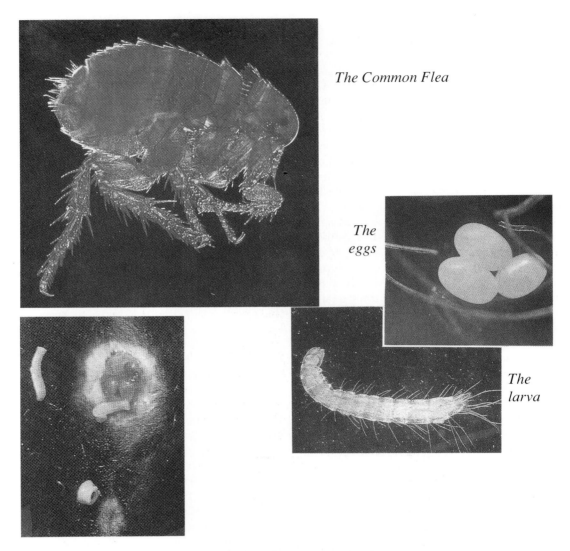

The Common Flea

The eggs

The larva

Tape Worm segments

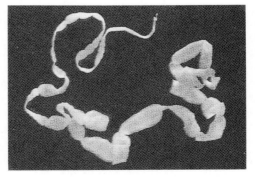

The Tape Worm can reach lengths of up to 20 inches.

Another source of tapeworm infestation is from a dog eating raw sheep's tripe, as the sheep eat the segments from the sheepdogs' faeces; so do cook all paunch thoroughly.

Tapeworn is easy to get rid of, providing you worm regularly with a good wormer. There are many on the market, but with a Collie that is heavily infested Droncit is perfect for the job. After your dog has been wormed for tapeworm, you must dispose of the stools, and burning is the best solution. Make sure you wash your hands thoroughly afterwards.

ECTOPARASITES
These are parasites which live outside the dog's body, usually on its skin.

FLEAS: These are the most common ectoparasites, and their life cycle is described above. Constant flea infestation causes allergic reaction and sores can develop around the flea bite mark. This, in turn, causes infection to set in. The easiest way to rid yourself and your Collie of this irritating parasite, is to spray regularly with one of the specially manufactured flea sprays. I recommend one that comes in two types: Nuvantop is designed to kill fleas on the dog, and Nuvanstay kills fleas in your home. There is a spray, called Acclaim, and this prevents eggs hatching into adult fleas.

TICKS: These parasites attach themselves to the animal and suck the blood until they are so full they eventually drop off. However, this can take quite a while, so do check your Collie for ticks. Most are picked up from fields near forested areas, or where there are deer or sheep. A tick can be removed by dabbing the affected area with a little surgical spirit. Never attempt to pull a tick off, as you will probably leave the mouth-piece still attached to the dog's skin.

CANINE AILMENTS
ALOPECIA
Loss of hair may be caused by many factors such as diet, fleas, mange, or an allergy to a shampoo. Some dogs worry at themselves, making bald patches, out of boredom. If loss of hair occurs, a visit to the vet is, hopefully, all that is needed. The source of the problem will be diagnosed, and the appropriate treatment will be prescribed.

ANAL GLANDS
Most Collies, Rough or Smooth, do not suffer with anal gland problems, but occasionally these glands, situated on either side of the anus, become too full. The Collie will drag its bottom along the ground, and it may constantly lick its rear end. If this happens, take your dog to the vet, who will perform the simple operation of emptying the glands. If this condition is left untreated, it can result in a nasty abscess. To prevent this problem from occurring, make sure your Collie has plenty of roughage in its diet, and plenty of exercise.

ARTIFICIAL RESPIRATION
It is useful to know what to do if your Collie stops breathing, due to shock or injury. If at all possible, lay the Collie on a table with its head hanging over the edge. Pull the tongue out of the mouth (out and forwards), and place your hand over the ribs and behind the shoulder blade to compress the chest, expelling the air in the lungs. Release the pressure and allow the chest to expand and fill with air. Compress the chest about twelve times within one minute. At this stage check the gums for colour. The dog will gasp and try to sit up. Try to keep your dog quiet and get it to the vet as soon as possible. You can also try mouth to nose resuscitation: close the Collie's mouth and blow very gently up the nose until the Collie starts to gasp and breathe.

ASTHMA
Any Collie with distressed breathing should be taken to the vet without delay. If your Collie is asthmatic, the treatment is the same as for humans, i.e. a course of Corticosteroids.

BAD BREATH
This may be caused by more than one factor. First check the teeth; bad breath could be caused by an accumulation of tartar or tooth decay. If the smell is very persistent, inform your vet, as the Collie could have a kidney malfunction. If this is the case, the vet will advise on the most appropriate form of treatment.

BALANITIS
This affects the penis, and it is caused by an infection in the mucous membrane of the sheath. It may be caused by simply lying on dirty ground. Wash around the area gently with mild antiseptic. If the condition persists, your vet may prescribe antibiotics. Sometimes a change of diet helps.

BLINDNESS
Collies, Rough or Smooth, may live to a very old age, and in some instances, a dog may go blind. This is not the end of the world: Collies have such acute hearing that this compensates to some extent. Blind dogs will find their way about on home ground with no trouble, providing no one puts obstacles in their path. It is most important that a blind dog is protected when it is taken away from its familiar surroundings; it could easily get lost and not return home, or even worse, it may be killed on the road, so do take care, and never leave a blind dog unattended outside the home.

BRUISING
If you suspect your Collie has been badly bruised, apply a cold compress. This will dilate the blood vessels and constrict the blood flow. As the compress is removed the blood flow increases, and so bruising heals faster.

BURNS AND SCALDS
If your Collie is unlucky enough to be burnt or scalded, speed is of the utmost importance. If possible, immerse the Collie in cold water to prevent the burn from penetrating further. Then take the dog to the vet so it can be treated for burns and for shock.

CLEFT PALATE
Puppies born with this deformity should be painlessly put to sleep by your vet. This must be done as soon as you notice the fault. Do not attempt to rear these puppies as most will die within a few weeks of being born as they cannot suckle well, and they become very weak.

COLLIE EYE ANOMALY (CEA)
It is a fact that a high percentage of Collies, Rough and Smooth, have Collie Eye Anomaly – this is not an exaggeration; it a fact. Collie Eye Anomaly is an ocular defect which is present at birth. One or more of several distinct and sometimes apparently unrelated features may be present in an affected eye. The most common is a bizarre arrangement of vessels underlying the retina, which is seen on the lateral side of the optic disc and is accompanied by a reduction in pigment. Other defects include pits in the optic disc or surrounding area and excessive tortuosity of the retinal vessels. Detachment of the retina and bleeding into the eye can develop in affected eyes. However, although CEA can be severe and cause total blindness, the defects are often so slight that neither dog nor owner are aware of the problem.

Most breeders are very careful with their breeding stock, and will only embark on a breeding programme using eye-tested stock.When you are buying a puppy, choosing a stud dog or buying a brood bitch check that it has been eye-tested and has been certified clear by a member of a panel of eye specialists. I am happy to say that more breeders are taking care regarding this problem, and if everyone eye-tested we would make progress towards eliminating the condition.

Mild CEA does not affect the Collie in its normal daily routine, and even if a Collie has a

CEA more severely, it will still be able to lead a useful life as a companion dog, providing there is no detachment of the retina. However, when affected stock is bred from, the puppies may be born blind, and I am sure no caring breeder wishes to be responsible for this heartache.

COLLIE NOSE
Fortunately, we do not see so much of this condition nowadays.The skin on the nose becomes crusted and very sore; it is also quite painful for the Collie. This problem is often caused by bright sunlight in the summer, and on bright snowy days in the winter. It is caused by ultra violet rays, and often causes scarring. If your Collie has a suspect Collie nose allergy, try using a barrier cream, and do not let your Collie sit in the bright sunlight too long. This problem is very difficult to overcome, and even after treatment, it may well reoccur.

COUGHING
The most common coughing in youngsters is often due to the fact they need worming. It could also be that the Collie has something caught in its throat. A dry, persistent cough is a nightmare in a large breeding establishment, as this usually means that the dogs have got kennel cough. If this is the case, isolate the dogs that are coughing, and contact your vet immediately. He will provide you with antibiotics, which are very effective. Beware of elderly Collies catching this disease, as it could be fatal. A throaty cough in an older Collie is often a sign of heart trouble.

CONSTIPATION
Unless the Collie is ill – and in this case speak to your vet – the safest laxative to use is a little liquid paraffin added to the Collie's dinner. This problem can be prevented by feeding a good diet with plenty of roughage. Make sure there is always access to fresh water.

CONTAGIOUS DISEASES
If you have any suspicion that your Collie may

have contacted some contagious type of illness, telephone your vet before going to the surgery, so you do not come into contact with any other dogs. It is very unfair to put other dogs at risk during normal surgery hours. By the same token, when you take a puppy to be vaccinated, always leave it in the car until it is your turn. You do not want to risk the puppy catching any infection, and the surgery floor cannot be washed after every consultation.

CUTS AND ABRASIONS
Cuts and abrasions can be caused by many factors, such as barbed wire, broken glass, etc. If the wound is small and open, just bathe with some very mild antiseptic such as savlon, and keep an eye on the wound for a few days. If the wound is much more open, such as a tear, it may need a few stitches. In this instance, wrap a bandage on to stop the flow of blood and take your Collie to the vet as soon as possible. A puncture wound is quite small, but all the more reason for a visit to your vet, as germs are carried into the wound and it is liable to become infected.

CYSTITIS
This is an infection of the urinary system and can often be very painful; in some cases blood is passed in the urine. Prompt treatment with antibiotics will soon solve the problem.

DIARRHOEA
For non-specific diarrhoea, starve the dog for at least twelve to twenty-four hours, and give a little water at frequent intervals. If you allow your Collie to drink too much, it will make matters worse. The idea is to get as much fluid into your Collie, a saucerful at a time. After starving the dog, feed a very bland diet for a few days. If the diarrhoea persists, contact your vet.

ECLAMPSIA
This condition is due to lack of calcium in a nursing bitch. It is most likely to occur in the

third week after whelping, although it can also occur during whelping. The bitch will suddenly show a changed attitude towards you and the puppies. She will become very restless, and she will shiver as if she is cold. She may have a glazed look in her eyes, and she may even have convulsions and go into a coma.

To prevent this condition from occurring, calcium should be given in low doses at the start of pregnancy, building up to a full dose at the time of whelping. A diet of good, nourishing food throughout the pregnancy will also help. If your bitch shows signs of eclampsia while nursing a litter, the puppies should be taken away from her, and the vet should be called straightaway.

ENTERITIS
Enteritis is a much more serious condition than ordinary diarrhoea. It entails inflammation of the bowel, loss of appetite and vomiting, followed by excessive thirst. Enteritis can be caused by a chill, by swallowing decomposed food stolen from the bin or by swallowing a foreign object, such as a toy. You must take your Collie to the vet, who will usually prescribe antibiotics. Warmth and rest is most important, and do not feed at all while the dog is vomiting. Make sure plenty of fluids are available, offered little and often. When your dog is recovering, feed a light diet for a few days.

ENTROPION
This is seldom seen in Collies, Rough or Smooth. The condition involves the in-turning of the upper or lower eyelid, or both; it may be unilateral or bilateral. The cause is commonly hereditary and can be noticed as early as four weeks of age. It can also be associated with an injury. Treatment is surgical, but is best left until the dog is least six months of age.

FALSE PREGNANCY
Sometimes called phantom pregnancy. Some bitches are prone to having false pregnancies.

This is not due to an excess of maternal feeling; it is the result of a hormone imbalance, and the bitch will need veterinary treatment. Some bitches come into full lactation at this time. If this occurs, you should cut out any extra food and make sure the bitch has plenty of exercise and is kept busy. She may become very broody and uncomfortable, and so if your Collie has a tendency to having phantom pregnancies, it is advisable to have her spayed.

HEART ATTACK
A heart attack may resemble a fainting fit, and may last for a few seconds or a few minutes. Older Collies are more prone, especially if the dog is overweight.

HEAT STROKE
Dogs cannot tolerate extremely hot weather, and great care should be taken that a dog is never left in a car without ventilation. It may not seem like a hot day, but the temperature soon builds up in a confined space. A dog suffering from heatstroke will pant excessively and its breathing will become laboured. In extreme cases, it may suffer a heart attack. In all cases of heatstroke, the dog's temperature must be lowered as quickly as possible. This can be done by applying ice packs or frozen food from the freezer to the dog's body. A small piece of ice placed in the rectum will also work rapidly. If no ice is available, immerse the dog in water – but do act quickly, as speed is essential.

HIP DYSPLASIA
This is a hereditary fault caused by the deformity of the hip joint, which is a ball and socket joint. If, for any reason, either the ball part of the joint or the socket part does not fit perfectly, arthritis, pain, and lameness can result. It is advisable to have your Collies X-rayed and hip-scored. If all breeders had their Collies hip-scored and did not breed those with a poor hip score, this would be beneficial to the breed.

MANGE (DERMODECTIC)
This is often caused by a breakdown in immunity in young puppies. Some pups grow out of this problem quite easily, while others may need a prolonged course of treatment.

MANGE (SARCOPTIC)
Mange mites burrow under the skin, causing intense irritation. Dogs that are constantly scratching should be looked at very closely to see if this is the problem. The mites are normally found on the ears and under the thighs. The skin in between the toes often becomes reddish brown in colour. Your vet will give you treatment to eradicate the mites, and this must be followed up by burning the Collie's bedding and thoroughly scrubbing the area where the Collie has been. If possible, the affected dog should be isolated, as this is a very persistent bug. If left too long without some form of treatment, the area will become unsightly and very sore.

MASTITIS
This is an inflammation of the mammary glands, during and after pregnancy. It can be very painful, and can result in an abscess forming. Early symptoms are a hardening round the teats. Quite often, puppies will not suckle from these teats, so if you are observant you can catch this painful condition in its early stages. Mastitis is often caused by a build-up of milk. Sometimes a bitch may make too much milk for tiny newborn pups to suckle, and this causes the teats to go hard and lumpy. At this stage the pups will not suckle at all from the affected teat, causing an even bigger build-up of milk. This often results in an abscess forming on or near the nipple. Antibiotics are used to clear up this condition, and this treatment will not affect the puppies in any way. If left untreated, the pups will drink milk that has been infected and will soon become ill.

OSTEOCHONDRITIS DISSECANS (OCD)
This is a generalised skeletal condition that is a degenerative process. It affects the growth plate cartilage as well as the articular cartilage of joints. This is usually seen in large breeds, but it has been reported in the Collie, Rough and Smooth. It is reported that the condition affects more males than females. It is caused by a number of factors, such as rapid growth, nutritional excesses such as diet imbalance, hormonal imbalance, trauma, and over-exercising young stock.

It is usually noticed at around four to eight months of age. The signs to look for are stiffness of the joints after resting or exercise, and the affected joint can be quite tender to touch. The term 'Osteochondritis' refers to an inflammatory reaction which develops in the joint, and the term 'Dissecans' relates to the cracks which develop in the articular cartilage to produce a separate fragment of cartilage, which forms a flap or loose body within the joint. In layman's terms, this means that cracks occur from the deep layers to the joint surface and synovial fluid passes along these cracks to reach the subchondral bone. Necrotic material also passes through these cracks to reach the joint cavity where mild inflammatory changes occur. The affected cartilage thickens because normal ossification does not occur, and the cartilage grows without being reabsorbed, it becomes necrotic in its deepest layers. Analgesics are usually prescribed and if no improvement occurs over a period of six weeks, surgery would be advised.

PANCREATIC INSUFFICIENCY
If your Collie ever has foul-smelling, fatty stools, loss of weight, a harsh, staring coat, and lack of animation, this may be the result of pancreatic problems. This deficiency of the digestive enzyme often produces foul-smelling stools. The condition can be controlled by treating the dog's food with pancreatic capsules, or if you have contact with a reputable slaughterhouse, you may be able to obtain some raw pig's pancreas. This problem can run in family lines. Sometime dogs grow

out of the problem, but others may well have to be on medication all their lives. I am happy to say this problem rarely occurs in Collies.

PROGRESSIVE RETINAL ATROPHY

In generalised progressive retinal atrophy the retina undergoes a form of degeneration which is seen through the ophthalmoscope as an accumulation of dark (pigment) spots over the tapetum lucidum. Signs of the disease are unlikely to appear in any breed before one year of age. At first only the central retina is affected, but the area gradually increases to include virtually the whole of the retina. Initially, vision is better peripherally than centrally; also, vision tends to be better in dull rather than bright light.

This condition is hereditary, and it is present in both the Rough and the Smooth Collie. If your dog carries the gene for PRA then it will develop it in spite of any special feeding or treatment. The condition will not improve and by definition will progress until the dog is blind. The special scheme run by the British Veterinary Association and the Kennel Club includes PRA, and certificates for clear dogs can be obtained under this scheme. It is most important that affected dogs and bitches should not be used for breeding. This action has already reduced the incidence quite markedly in both the Border Collie and the Labrador.

PYOMETRA

An accumulation of pus in the uterus could lead to a condition known as Pyometra. This is an infection of the womb caused by a hormone imbalance, and if it is not treated, it can be fatal.

HOMOEOPATHIC MEDICINES

Increasingly, there are those who prefer to use natural medicines to treat themselves and their pets. The following remedies are for common ailments only, and should never be used without first consulting a homoeopathic practitioner. Homoeopathy is the practice of treating an illness with a substance that produces the same symptoms that are presented by the animal or person that is ill. Homoeopathy has been known and used since around 500 BC, and in the late 18th century it was widely used in all walks of life. Animals respond well to homoeopathy, and one of the great advantages it has over conventional medicine is that does not produce any dangerous side effects. All health stores and chemists sell homoeopathic medicine, and it is very easy to use.

Here are a few useful medicines to keep in your medical box. Please bear in mind that if your Collie shows any sign of illness, it is most important to seek the advice of a good vet. Any change in your dog's behaviour could be a sign that all is not well, and an observant owner can sometimes prevent their dog from suffering a major illness by spotting a problem in its early stages.

ACONITE Travel sickness.
APIS MEL Insect bites.
ARGENT NIT Colic and flatulence.
ARNICA Bruises, sprains – use after any small injury for shock.
ARSEN ALB Loss of appetite.
BELLADONNA Heat stroke.
CALC FLUOR Incontinence in older bitches.
CANTHARIS Cystitis (if symptoms persist see your vet).
CARBO VEG Bad breath and breaking of wind.
EUPHRASIA Hayfever.
GELSEMIUM Nervousness in show animals.
IGNATIA Pining due to loss of litter.
PHOSPHORUS Sensitivity to sudden noise (thunder or fireworks).
SEPIA Constipation during pregnancy.
SULPHUR Offensive smell.
THUJA Warty growths.

Before using alternative medicine, it is advisable to visit a vet who specialises in homoepathy, or to read some books on this subject; you will find most libraries stock a selection, and they make interesting reading.

WHEN TO CALL THE VET

As I work in a very busy veterinary practice, I can assure you first hand, that vets are not amused if they are called out in the middle of the night for a trivial whim – Lassie's nails do not *need* trimming on Christmas Day even if its claws are catching on the new carpet! On the other hand, never be afraid to call out your vet in the night for anything that may be serious – that is what a vet is for.

If your dog has an accident, or is suddenly taken very ill, telephone straightaway. If you get an answering machine, hang on, as your call may be diverted. The duty vet may be out on another call, so listen carefully to any message given. Try not to panic, but speak in a very clear voice, giving your name and telephone number, and try to explain the symptoms your dog is showing.

EMERGENCIES

There are certain diseases or accidents which require emergency treatment. These include:

BLOAT The dog is in pain with its stomach full of gas. If you suspect bloat, contact your vet straightaway, as no time must be lost, or the results may well be fatal. Bloat can be prevented by feeding two meals a day instead of one big meal, and never allowing your Collie to drink masses of water after a meal, or to take excessive exercise. Full bloat or Torsion will mean an operation.

EYE INJURIES First apply a cold wet cloth, and then take your Collie to the surgery straightaway. Try to stop the Collie from rubbing the injured eye.

POISONING Take the dog to the surgery at once if poisoning is suspected. If possible, bring any evidence relating to the cause of poisoning, such as bottles, packets etc., so that the vet knows how to treat the dog.

DOG FIGHTS Unless large, gaping wounds are evident, and as long as there is no heavy loss of blood, these wounds can often wait until normal surgery times. Clean up the surrounding area, as sometimes the wounds look worse than they really are.

HOW TO ASSIST YOUR VET

Try to keep a case history of your Collie, noting any health problems, keeping a check when its inoculations are due, and, if it is a bitch, noting when seasons are due, so you will know if anything is abnormal. If you have a bitch in whelp, always inform your vet prior to the whelping date, in case help is needed. Build a good relationship with your vet and his staff – they could be your Collie's lifeline.

CARE OF THE OLD COLLIE

One of the most important aspects of keeping Collies, Rough or Smooth, is the care of your old-timers. Collies have a good life-span, and some are still very active at thirteen and fourteen years old. With a little extra thought, and a little extra care, you can make life easier and more comfortable for the elderly dog.

An old dog cannot tolerate extremes of temperature, so never leave your old Collie out too long on a cold, wet day, or in very hot weather. Inoculation boosters should be kept up to date; your dog is still at risk from infection, even if it does not go out. Teeth decay may cause problems, so keep a check on your dog's mouth. If it is suffering from bad breath, it could be the result of bad teeth, and these will need to be removed.

Do not overfeed; most elderly dogs will be better suited by a couple of small meals a day, instead of one big meal. A little margarine or corn oil on the food will help to prevent the coat from becoming dry. Older Collies will have a better appetite if you slightly warm the food; fresh cooked chicken, or fish with rice is most appetising. This may sound slightly extravagant – but why not? Your Collie has given you many years of pleasure; now it is your turn to make its last years a pleasure to you both. A nice, thoughtful gesture is to raise your old Collie's water bowl from the ground to make drinking easier.

An old dog is likely to rest a lot more, and so its bed is very important. Make sure the bed is soft to ease the old bones, and it should be kept clean and dry, and most importantly it should be free from draughts. Most old Collies become rather restless, but reassurance, and a bit of loving attention, will help to settle them. If your Collie should go blind with age, it will still be able to cope fairly well in the house that it knows, providing no new obstacles are placed in the way – so avoid any plans to reorganise the furniture.

When your Collie's time comes, let it go with dignity and before it loses all its faculties. The Collie is a proud dog, and would not want to be a burden. Inform your vet of your wishes, and ask if you may make a special appointment outside normal surgery hours. No one will mind if you have a good cry – I have seen great big men cry over the loss of their beloved dog, and you will find the vet and staff most helpful at a time like this. Many surgeries offer a cremation service, and I personally think this is the best and final act of love you can give your Collie.

Go home and think of all the good times you shared with your Collie – the shows, the long walks, and those times sitting in front of the fire on long winter nights, when a muzzle sneaks into your hand, and those lovely eyes look up at you. Give thanks for the shared pleasure of having owned this breed – the magnificent Collie.